Part of the Magic

of the

Magic

A Collection of
DISNEY-INSPIRED
Brushes with Greatness

Bambi Moé

University Press of Mississippi / Jackson

The University Press of Mississippi is the scholarly publishing agency of
the Mississippi Institutions of Higher Learning: Alcorn State University,
Delta State University, Jackson State University, Mississippi State University,
Mississippi University for Women, Mississippi Valley State University,
University of Mississippi, and University of Southern Mississippi.

www.upress.state.ms.us

The University Press of Mississippi is a member
of the Association of University Presses.

Illustrations courtesy of the author

First printing 2023
∞

Library of Congress Control Number 2023006223
Hardback ISBN 978-1-4968-4423-1
Epub single ISBN 978-1-4968-4424-8
Epub institutional ISBN 978-1-4968-4425-5
PDF single ISBN 978-1-4968-4426-2
PDF institutional ISBN 978-1-4968-4427-9

British Library Cataloging-in-Publication Data available

Contents

Prologue

An invisible thread connects those who are destined to meet, regardless of time, place, or circumstance. The thread may stretch or tangle, but it will never break. May you be open to each thread that comes into your life—the golden ones and the coarse ones—and may you weave them into a brilliant and beautiful life.

—Ancient Chinese proverb

During an interview, a journalist once asked me, "What do you think makes you good at your job?" At the time, I said I did not know the answer. Upon reflection, I suspect it had something to do with the deep connection I felt to the words and music of the singer-songwriter. As far back as I can remember, I always thought songwriters were magicians. Writing songs and telling stories with their words seemed mystical to me. The singer-songwriter possessed the power to heal your heart and transcend feelings of isolation and loneliness, and music has always played an integral part in my life.

I studied and read album jackets and liner notes as if they were library books. My first job was working in a record store for Wherehouse Records in Santa Monica, California. My interest in the art form exceeded being a fan of music. It was my passion. I researched and investigated the names that appeared on record labels. I would test my knowledge by listening to a song and delighted myself when I could name the artist and the songwriter. In fact, I often identified the musicians who played on the record as well. Whether it was Carole King's "It's Too Late" or Joni Mitchell's "Free Man in Paris" or Joan Baez's "Jesse" or anything by the Beatles, I felt I had found kindred spirits and a connection to a family of musical troubadours. I had no way of knowing then that my musical interests would provide me with tools I would later use in my career at The Walt Disney Company.

The ultimate test came during my Disney job interview. After I answered a series of questions, Tom Bocci, the manager of Disney Music Publishing, played two songs for me. He said that both songs were under consideration for a new Disney film called *The Devil and Max Devlin*. The first song I heard was "Roses and Rainbows." Tom asked me to share my impressions. I told him, "It would make a great end title song because it was up-tempo and lyrically upbeat, a feel-good kind of song, one you would hear during the credit roll as you were exiting a movie theater." I thought I heard Tom say "huh" under his breath as he played the next song, "Any Fool Could See." Upon hearing the ballad for the first time, I got so excited because I immediately recognized the singer. I said, "Is that Julie Budd?" This time I clearly heard Tom say something about having "good ears and maybe some luck." Perhaps he was right. Not only did I get the job, but I was lucky enough to have a lifetime's worth of the most amazing brushes with greatness.

Acknowledgments

For Elizabeth

To my mom Elvira—thank you for sharing your love of all things Disney.

For Walter and Darla Moe and my siblings Eric, Lance, and Gretchen.

Under the category of "I couldn't have done it without you" THANK YOU Shannon Farnon, Linda Edell Howard, Julie Enzer, Laurel Whitcomb, Marc Perlman, Cheryl Davis, Phil Savenick, Greg Ehrbar, Lisa Ynda Coleman, The Secor Family, Mark Watters, Mary Jo Mennella, Lisa Dobbyn Hubbard, Basem and Anna Wasef, Susan Hartmann, Rocci Chatfield, Heather Musso, Elisa Garcia Hasluck, Bruce Cranston, Patty and Michael Silversher, Paula Sigman Lowery, Eric Roberts, Rita Berger, Janalyn Glymph, Sabrina Fair Thomas, Skypp Cabanas, Michael Todd, Kevin DeRemer, Nathan DeRemer, Rick Markovitz, Darrin Banks, Lauren Wood, Sarah Douglas, Zak Barnett, Matthew Serrano, Jymn Magon, Adam Berry, Stephen James Taylor, Gary Krisel, Gaby Michel, Thom Rollerson, The Jefferds Family, Craig Gill, Lisa Carey, Jill Schultz, Tom Caltabiano, Jennifer Hegarty, Kia Kamran, Tamara Sobel, Howard Green, Heather Blodget, Leah Latham, Michael Lyons, Anne Thompson, Paula Bonhomme, Kevin Miller, The Rorman Family, and David "Z" Rivkin.

Part of the Magic

What Is a Brush with Greatness?

A brush with greatness is like a photographic moment in time. There is a captured richness and quality to the storytelling experience, in the same way a photo encapsulates a memory. It is a reflected-on part of a life's journey. A brush is an event, and it is rarely a trivial encounter. The beauty of a brush with greatness is that it is always a shared moment between two or more people. It is undeniable and serves to remind us of our connectivity by virtue of our humanity. A brush with greatness, or BWG, can happen to anyone, anywhere, at any time. The only rule, if there is one, is that a real brush is a meaningful encounter, which is a great deal more than just a sighting.

There are all kinds of BWGs. There are *double* brushes or *triple* brushes when you have multiple encounters with the same person. There are *unknown* brushes when you don't know you have had one until long after the fact. And there are *shared* brushes, which are my personal favorites, because they are the ones you experience with a friend or loved one.

Brushes can fall into all categories of encounters, including those you wish you didn't have.

Regardless of the kind of brush, we are all part of a cultural revolution of universal connectivity. Stories told through a multitude of devices and screens provide an outlet for limitless self-expression. Our ancient ancestors believed that the quality of one's life can and will be measured by the stories we have to tell. Our stories, which include our brushes with greatness, will live on long after we are gone. The joy of a BWG extends far beyond the original encounter and multiplies in the retelling of the story. In a way, our brushes become an inspirational gift that keeps on giving. Sharing our stories is the only way to prevent them from being lost.

Many of my anecdotal stories contain the names of a number of well-known figures and center on my career at The Walt Disney Company. This was not by design or purpose, and every brush with greatness is true, based on the way I remember it. I hope that when I share my stories, whether humorous, profound, heartbreaking, or deeply personal, you will be inspired to share your own.

While writing this book, I was reminded of a song lyric from *Mary Poppins*: "A man has dreams of walking with giants, to carve his niche in the edifice of time." For me a brush with greatness is the expression of my gratitude for so many of my dreams coming true while walking with giants.

Chapter 1

I Think I'll Call Her Bambi

While living in New York, my mother worked as a Barbizon bathing suit model. She was beautiful in an Audrey Hepburn kind of way. She came from a large Italian family and had five sisters and a brother. She was second to the youngest and made her way out to the West Coast after joining the Army Reserve. Her boyfriend at the time was a well-known studio photographer, and he took the photo of her that appears at the end of this chapter. My father, an immigrant from Germany, worked at Ideal Toys as an inventor and sidelined as a musician. A graduate of Hamburg University, my father loved to play the drums and started a dance band. He too had movie star good looks and, I would guess, quite a few female admirers. At Ideal Toys, my father worked alongside Rube Goldberg on the classic game *Mouse Trap* and the original *Mr. Machine*.

Separately, my future parents each set their sights on Hollywood. They met on a blind date, and a whirlwind courtship led to marriage in the famed Little White Wedding Chapel in Las Vegas.

My *earliest* brush with greatness almost happened while I was still in my mother's womb. On October 2, 1957, my parents were on their way to a Hollywood premiere at Universal Studios. My mother, nearly nine months pregnant, could not have asked for a more thrilling invitation. They were there to see a film called *Slim Carter*, starring Jock Mahoney of *Tarzan* fame. Both parents were big fans of Jock Mahoney, and my mother later told me about the time she met the hunky actor at a parade when he became honorary sheriff of Encino, California. With klieg lights flashing into the night sky, my parents made their way onto the red carpet and into a packed theatre. Just as the lights dimmed and the film was about to start, my mother's water broke. I was on the verge of making my own debut.

Fortunately for all concerned, the West Valley hospital where I was born was just a short ten-mile drive on the 101 freeway to Encino. I wonder if Sheriff Mahoney would have provided a motorcade escort if he had not been at his own Hollywood movie premiere.

Suddenly my parents had an important decision to make: what to name their baby daughter?

Perhaps my auspicious birth had signaled my future in show business, but it was my name that certainly sealed the deal.

Bambi was a name my parents knew from the Disney film. However, this was 1957, and the popular trend of naming children after animated characters had not caught on yet. There were other baby names under consideration, and for some reason never told to me, all the names started with the letter *B*: Betty Jo, Billie Jo, and Bobbie Jo. The final decision to name me Bambi had to do with *Your Show of Shows*, and the show's beautiful blonde-haired, blue-eyed dancer-choreographer named Bambi Linn. My folks thought that if there was one person named Bambi, and a beautiful one at that, then why not name their daughter the same? I am certain that they gave little consideration to the fact that the animated deer named Bambi was a boy and I am neither blonde haired nor blue-eyed. My sweet but unusual name led to a good deal of teasing and bullying while I was growing up. There were times in my life when I thought about changing it. I wondered if it would make a difference when first meeting someone. I would have welcomed not becoming the butt of another deer joke or crass comment about a stripper.

Slim Carter movie poster

Cliff Edwards

Doreen Kohut, one of Walt Disney's secretaries at the time of my birth, happened to be a close family friend. When she heard that my parents had named me Bambi, she made sure to commemorate the event and asked Mr. Disney to sign a serigraph of the famous thicket scene with the butterfly on Bambi's tail. Mr. Disney obliged, and he wrote "To Bambi Moé with Best Wishes—Walt Disney." A picture of the serigraph appears at the end of the chapter. I had no idea what a treasure this was until many years later. I brought the signed serigraph into work one day and asked Dave Smith, the legendary Disney archivist, to look it over. He suggested that I have it framed by the Disney art props department. Dale Alexander, who was department head, took one look at it and said he had the perfect frame. Dale told me that Mr. Disney gave serigraphs like mine as gifts to visiting dignitaries and VIPs. When Dale returned it to me, it was in one of the original blond wood frames. My mother cried tears of joy when she saw it.

We rarely spoke about it, but my mother's love of all things Disney, and specifically Mickey Mouse, was a constant presence throughout her life. Mickey symbolized hope and provided humor during her

Depression-era childhood. So it's not surprising to me that my family lived in a garden apartment on Buena Vista Street in Burbank, a mere block away from the Walt Disney Studios. I barely remember it as a sleepy community of ground-floor bungalow apartments. Each apartment had a screen door that faced another apartment, separated by a garden courtyard and concrete pathway. One of our neighbors was a well-known voice actor who worked in animation. He got a kick out of my parents naming me Bambi. I knew him as Mr. Edwards, the nice man who used to make me laugh by making up funny voices, and sometimes he gave me gifts for no other reason than it was a Friday. My four- or five-year-old self would occasionally wait by the door for him to come home, just so I could ask him to play his ukulele and sing me a silly song. I will never forget the time he brought me my very favorite toy: a battery-operated Bongo the Bear on roller skates. Bongo had a tiny red cap on his head, and I spent many hours watching him skate up and down our pathway.

Years later, my mother told me that this kind, soft-spoken man was Cliff Edwards, the beloved voice of Jiminy Cricket, Pinocchio's conscience and my friend. He was my first *unknown* brush with greatness, and like all firsts, my encounter with Mr. Edwards holds a special place in my heart, and I will never forget it.

In a way, my name helped me to develop my sense of humor and not take myself too seriously. I had to laugh the night I went on a class field trip with the Santa Monica College Theatre Arts Department to the Ahmanson Theatre in Los Angeles to see the Neil Simon play *Chapter Two*. At one point in the show, a character is introduced as Bambi and described as having big boobs along with wearing electric silver go-go boots. All of a sudden, a roar of laughter broke out in different sections of the theatre. My best friend, sitting next to me, gave me the elbow as we both chuckled and my face turned beet red. However, it is still amusing when someone tells me that my name suits me; it must be my big brown eyes. The name stuck, and my connection to The Walt Disney Company was fated.

My father on the drums

My mother during her modeling days

Bambi serigraph signed by Walt Disney

Chapter 2

Holy Family

The remarkable thing about a BWG is that sometimes you can have one and not know it until years later. This happened to me when I was in high school. My parents had gotten divorced, and my father remarried. My brother Eric and I spent time shuttling back and forth between two households in Long Island, New York, one in Plainview and the other in Huntington. My new stepmother, Elizabeth, a former graduate of Fontbonne Hall Academy, a Roman Catholic girls' school, proposed that I attend Holy Family High School, near our Huntington home. I was not a big fan of wearing a uniform, but I heard the school had a great theatre arts department led by Charles Klute, and I hoped to audition for the upcoming school production of *Auntie Mame*.

One of the coolest things I remember about attending Holy Family is that every day as I walked to school, I passed the historic home that Fanny Brice shared with Nick Arnstein. As a self-proclaimed theatre geek, I knew that those names were part of theatre royalty, thanks to Barbra Streisand and her portrayal of Fanny Brice in *Funny Girl*.

One day on my way to school, I noticed a "For Sale / Open House" sign in the front yard of the property. I knew I had to convince my father and stepmother to pose as potential buyers and take me with them. Once inside, I excitedly went from room to room until I made a great discovery. In an upstairs attic space, I found a small, kid-size door, and barely squeezing through, I found myself inside an elaborate dollhouse. It was a replica of one of the rooms in the main house with a sign posted that read "Grownups Keep Out." It was surprisingly roomy and made a great hide-and-seek hiding place. Fortunately, I have never lost my childlike curiosity about most things in life.

The theatre bug had bitten me at a young age after I saw my first off-Broadway musical, *The Me Nobody Knows*, based on a collection of stories by city kids between the ages of seven and eighteen and their feelings about life in their neighborhoods. The show starred Beverly Bremers and the then-unknown future star of *Fame*, Irene Cara, who played the role of Coco Hernandez in the film and sang the title song. Not only did I relate to the story, but I also loved the groundbreaking musical score. I performed the song "Dream Babies" from the show at my singing audition to get into Mr. Klute's class and landed the part of the Bougainvillea Girl in *Auntie Mame*. Thrilled at having even the smallest part, I immersed myself in school, and thanks to Mr. Klute, I had multiple brush experiences.

Mr. Klute organized a class field trip to New York City to see a show at the famed Shubert Theatre. The play was a musical called *Over Here!*, and the score was written by Richard M. and Robert B. Sherman. My love of the Sherman Brothers and their music began with their score for *Mary Poppins*. The film had a deep and profound effect on me, having endured my parents' divorce, and I had no way of knowing then that the Sherman Brothers and I would collaborate on several projects and ultimately become friends.

As an added field trip surprise, Mr. Klute had arranged to have his friend John meet us at the stage door and give us a tour of the historic theatre.

I was barely seventeen at the time, yet I remembered thinking how cute John was—even with a bad case of acne. I hung on his every word. John told us that the Shubert had opened in 1913, and he showed us where the stage trap doors were and how the floor hydraulics worked. One of his first roles was in the play *Over Here!*, and he said he was so excited to be working with the legendary 1940s icons the Andrews Sisters, Maxine and Patty.

No self-respecting theatre geek would be without a *Playbill* collection, and several years later, while looking through mine, I noticed three autographs on the front cover of my program for *Over Here!* I recognized Maxine and Patty Andrews's signatures, but not the third name. I do remember seeing one of the other actors in the show leaving the stage door, and I went up to him and asked him to sign my program. He was handsome and had twinkly eyes. It tickled me to discover that my crush had been on Treat Williams, star of Broadway's *Hair* and TV's *Everwood*. I met him years later at an Emmy Awards "For Your Consideration" event, and I gave him my extra copy of the show program. He seemed flattered by my acknowledgment of his earlier work.

Over Here! featured performances by several other notable names, including Marilu Henner of TV's *Taxi* fame and the actor Samuel E. Wright. In what would appear to be another Disney twist of fate, Sam Wright and I would cross paths years later when he voiced the character of Sebastian the crab in Disney's *The Little Mermaid*.

However, the most shocking brush was finding out that Mr. Klute's friend John, our cute blemished actor–tour guide, was in fact John Travolta. Once I got over the shock, I realized I actually had a *crush* with greatness.

Another interesting aspect of a BWG is how it can reveal a link between people, places, and events that may appear as an invisible thread when reflecting back on one's life. Not only did I clearly have a Disney connection, but I also had an unexpected encounter with the woman who had inspired my love of musicals through her performance in *The Me Nobody Knows*.

When I was working at Disneyland / Vista Records on a children's song album called *Mousercise*, we put out a casting call for

Playbill featuring the Andrews Sisters' *Over Here*

Everwood promotional postcard featuring Treat Williams

potential theme songs, and I noticed the name of a songwriter who had submitted a main title theme. Seeing the name Beverly Bremers, I decided to call and ask if she was the same Beverly Bremers from my childhood memory. We had a lovely conversation, and she told me how touched she was by my fond recollection of her and her inspiring performance in *The Me Nobody Knows*. It is hard to say for sure, but I wonder if I had not seen *The Me Nobody Knows* and been so moved by Beverly's performance, would I have picked out her tape from the hundreds of submissions? Maybe it was a happy accident, but Beverly wound up writing the theme music for *Mousercise*, and it earned us both a gold record.

Sometimes the initial brush can act as a catalyst for a greater connection or purpose. At least that is how it has worked for me.

Playbill featuring *The Me Nobody Knows*, with Beverly Bremers note

Gold record awarded to me for my work on *Mousercise*

Chapter 3

Watch Out for Guys with Black Ears

By the time I enrolled at Santa Monica College, my apparent connection to The Walt Disney Company no longer took me by surprise. I knew it was more than just my name as I kept discovering invisible threads.

Meeting my future best friend Jeanie Jefferds for the first time was like bearing witness to a force of nature. Standing on the steps of the school's outdoor amphitheater at a lunchtime performance by Gil Scott-Heron in the quad, I saw a woman with long, curly, light-brown hair and colorful bell-bottom pants swaying as she danced with reckless abandon to the music. It was hard not to notice the Nikon camera dangling precariously from her neck. What a free spirit, I thought. I found out later that the camera was not just an accessory; she was covering the concert for the school paper. I introduced myself, and she laughed. Expecting to hear another deer joke, I said, "What is so funny?" With a wink and a smile, she replied, "My dad works at Disney." From that moment on, Jeanie and I were as inseparable as Bambi and Thumper, which ultimately became her endearing nickname.

One *inspirational* BWG unlike any other holds a very special place in my heart. It is my most personal one, and it literally helped shape my life and career in the entertainment business. It was with a man named Vincent Jefferds.

Mr. Jefferds was the head of Consumer Products, one of the most profitable divisions at The Walt Disney Company. He was a top creative marketing executive who played a key role in the growth and development of one of the largest entertainment companies in the world, and as legend has it, he made a name for himself by coming up with the marketing and sales of the Davy Crockett coonskin cap. To many who knew him, he was feared and revered. A boxer in his youth, Vince Jefferds was a fine artist and a collector of fine art, an author of more than two dozen children's books, an avid tennis player, and a celebrated figure in the publishing world.

Vince Jefferds was not just my best friend Jeanie's dad; he was a father and mentor to me. True, he was gruff and bearlike in his approach to most things, including his daughter's friends, but I always knew where I stood with him, and I think he liked that I was not afraid of him. I loved listening to his stories and insights about the entertainment business. He would often argue about why one film became a box office success versus another film that he enjoyed more. You could always count on a lively conversation in the living room with his friends like Jennings Lang, (producer of the blockbuster disaster films *Airport* and *Earthquake*), Academy Award–winning actor Max von Sydow, and best-selling author-screenwriter Ray Bradbury, as well as so many others. Without his ever saying it, I knew he had a great fondness for Card Walker, the head of Disney Productions, and counted Fess Parker, a.k.a. Davy Crockett, among his closest friends.

The tone of his voice would change when he talked about the future prosperity and growth of The Walt Disney Company. He spoke with confident authority, and I never heard arrogance or entitlement in his words. I admired his equal parts of passion and pride whether he was talking about the upcoming slate of Disney films or the potential expansion of the Disney theme parks or the newest Mickey Mouse merchandise. Like the true artist that he was, he painted a picture in my mind, and I wanted to be part of that world.

I spent a lot of time in the Jefferds home. Mama Jean, Vince's wife and Jeanie's mom, was always warm and welcoming. She loved a house full of activity and was the hostess with the mostest; you would not be in the house for five minutes without a drink in your hand and a plate of something delicious to eat. There was always a tennis match on the television or, more often than not, a competitive doubles match led by Mama Jean on the backyard court. Mr. and Mrs. Jefferds were a formidable couple. Mr. Jefferds could appear larger-than-life and somewhat unapproachable, yet he always had time to talk with me. He listened with the caring and loving ears of a father. His guidance was infused with a remarkable amount of patience and understanding.

In 1981, when I saw a job listing in the *Hollywood Reporter* for a copyright assistant in Music Publishing at Disneyland / Vista Records, I knew there was only one person to call: Mama Jean. I told her about the ad and wanted to know if the position had a typing requirement. I was afraid I might be too slow if given a typing test. She listened and then instructed me to call Mr. Jefferds's office to find out. When I made the appointment to meet with him, his assistant Vera chuckled when I said, "This is Bambi calling."

It was my first time on the Disney lot. With a sense of awe and anxiety, I remember thinking that the grounds looked like a college campus, with neatly trimmed hedges and nondescript buildings with lots of windows that looked out on rolling green grass and scampering squirrels. Then I got to the corner of Mickey Avenue and Dopey Drive—no kidding, there really is a street sign that lets you know where you are, just a few hundred yards away from a Mickey Mouse topiary, an actual hedge bearing the likeness of Mickey himself.

I told Mr. Jefferds what I knew about the job and why I thought I would be great for it. I had no idea that Disneyland / Vista Records was one small division under the large umbrella of Consumer

Vince Jefferds

Products and Mr. Jefferds's vast domain. It is fair to assume that knowing the big boss was a benefit. Mr. Jefferds called personnel and recommended me as a candidate for the open position. I could hardly believe the glowing endorsement I received from the man I looked up to and admired most. However, knowing the big boss meant that I had to work harder than anyone else and prove that I deserved the opportunity—if not to him, then definitely to myself.

Vincent H. Jefferds was an inspiring man of many talents. Through his belief in me, I got a chance to get my foot in the door and make a name for myself. I treasure the congratulatory drawing Mr. Jefferds made for me when I got the job. He drew a picture of

Mickey Mouse holding a paintbrush, and across the top of the page he wrote "Much love to Bambi," and below the drawing of Mickey, "Watch out for guys with black ears." In my heart, I know that Vince got a kick out of me sharing my Disney work adventures with him. In fact, the first record I ever produced at Disneyland / Vista Records was a Davy Crockett read-along book and record. It was a serendipitous assignment, and it would forever connect me work-wise to Mr. Jefferds. In the beginning, I struggled to fit in. It was important to me to have my work taken seriously, but my name and my connection to Mr. Jefferds did not help my situation. However, I knew how lucky I was to be starting my career at The Walt Disney Company.

My work-related brushes at Disney are vast in number and span many years. The stories that follow offer a behind-the-scenes look at being a Disney cast member and part of a magical team.

Chapter 4

Did You Change Your Name to Work There?

When I was hired as a copyright assistant in the Music Publishing department of Disneyland / Vista Records in February 1981, the first question everyone asked me was "did you change your name to work there?" Hmm, do people do that?

As you can imagine, I have heard virtually every deer joke ever thought of . . . "Got any doe?" "Hey! The buck stops here!" and the most popular, "You're such a deer." My name attracted all kinds of attention, including folks who called The Walt Disney Company looking for the four-legged animated creature whose name I shared. However, I could not have imagined my name would provide my next brush with greatness and, arguably, my most *legendary* one.

One day in November 1985, I got a call from my friend Teri. She was working for Rusty Lemorande, the producer of *Captain EO*, a 3D film ride attraction starring Michael Jackson. This was during the heyday of Michael Jackson's fame and popularity. Everyone at the company knew he was a major Disney fan. In fact, it was common to see Michael wandering around the Disney lot. Michael's favorite place to visit was the Studio Archives, an unofficial Disney museum of memorabilia. Rumor has it that he spent a lot of time there, researching plans to build his own version of Disneyland. He ultimately built a residence in Santa Barbara County. Paying homage to *Peter Pan*, he called it Neverland.

At first, studio chiefs Michael Eisner and Jeffrey Katzenberg liked having Michael Jackson around, but things got a bit out of hand, as employees were constantly leaving their workstations and offices, hoping to catch a glimpse of him.

Because of the workplace disruption, Michael's visits became covert. In the beginning, he would arrive through the front gate in a limousine, but he soon started going through the back gate in a beat-up station wagon. Some days he wore disguises. I worked in the same building as the archives, so I asked my friend Paula Sigman, who worked there, if she would ask Michael to autograph an old Jackson 5 record for me. The album was *Diana Ross Presents the Jackson 5*, and with a red crayon, he signed it "Love, Michael Jackson, 1998."

Then, on this particular day in November, I got *the* call. "Bambi, it's Teri. I know you won't believe this, but Michael Jackson wants to meet you." "Yeah, right," I said. "No, really, he heard that there was a real live person named Bambi who worked at Disney, and I told him I knew you." In complete disbelief, I said, "Come on, you're pulling my leg." "No, I swear I'm not, come to our office at 3 p.m. today, and I'll take you over to meet him."

Thinking I would outsmart her and prove she was trying to pull a fast one on me, I called the front gate to check with security to find out if Michael was on the lot that day. Unbeknownst to me, the guards had been instructed not to give out any information regarding Michael's whereabouts, and they responded by telling me, "No, he's not here today."

With my doubts confirmed, I calmly headed over at 3 p.m. to meet Teri. She rushed us right out the door. At some point, I figured she had to confess that this was a joke as we walked hurriedly toward the soundstages. I remember noticing a blockade and a security guard and a large motor-home-like trailer. Wow, I thought, my friend has really gone off the deep end as she instructed me to wait behind the barricade. I watched her go up to the motor home and knock on the door. What happened next is kind of a blur. I heard Teri say, "Please tell Michael that Bambi's here to see him," and then I heard that truly unmistakable voice say, "Tell Bambi I'll be with her in a minute." Before I had a moment to process what was happening, Teri quickly escorted me into the motor home.

There, in a white T-shirt and black jeans, stood Michael Jackson. Actually, he was so tall that he had to hunch over inside the trailer. He asked me to sit down across the table from him. Someone asked him, "Do you need anything?" and he said "no." It suddenly dawned on me that I was alone with the King of Pop.

I know it sounds odd, but I immediately noticed his fingers. They were really long and skinny. Then I saw he had a kind smile and a seemingly sweet and gentle nature. There was something very special about his energy. You could just feel it. Who knows, maybe there was something to it—because, after all, this was the man who, according to news reports, was about to buy the bones of the Elephant Man!

I remember that he went out of his way to put me at ease and engage me in conversation. He said he knew about *Totally Minnie*, the album I worked on. He mentioned that Jai Winding, who was the music director for the Jacksons' Victory Tour, had told him about it.

Michael appeared bright and interested and not at all like the person portrayed in the press. He asked me about my name and some of the projects we were working on. I got so comfortable that I started to talk with him about the business of making children's records. I told him, "You make my job really difficult." He laughed and asked me, "What do you mean by that?" I explained that our core Disney Records audience, the younger brothers and sisters of Michael's fan base, wanted pop-friendly hit music too. Michael asked me about the digital remix of the soundtrack to *Fantasia*. He said he had some kids on set with him and would love to get a couple of copies to share.

After what must have been at least twenty minutes to a half hour, someone knocked on the door and said, "Michael, they need you back on set." As we stood up, with our meeting about to end, I remember my heart skipping a beat as Michael Jackson leaned

Michael Jackson autograph, 1998

forward to kiss my cheek. Moreover, as if in slow motion I could not fully comprehend my own great good fortune, I grabbed both his hands and shook them as firmly as I could and said, "Nice to meet you." I remember racing back to the office and grabbing every copy of *Fantasia* I could find and telling anyone who was within earshot that I had just met with the one and only Michael Jackson.

By the time I got back to the trailer, Michael was gone, so I went inside the soundstage. Apparently they were there to reshoot a scene involving Anjelica Huston's feet. I remember clutching the albums to my chest, determined to present them to Michael myself. I thought that as long as I held on to them, I could stay and watch the filming, but as fate would have it, Michael's assistant approached me and asked if they were the albums for Michael, and I said "yes" as I reluctantly handed them over.

I stood in the same spot for several minutes as the large stage door opened behind me, flooding the room with light. I did not move a muscle, thinking it was a security guard about to ask me to

Michael Jackson autograph

leave. Trying my best to look as if I belonged there, and not wanting my brush with the King of Pop to end, I casually glanced over at the person now standing next to me. I momentarily lost my breath as I locked eyes with Elizabeth Taylor. In a whisper, as if talking to myself, I said, "It's you," and with an acknowledging nod she was quickly whisked away to see Michael.

Nearly twenty-two years later, I was working on the music for a Hallmark Hall of Fame production of *Riding the Bus with My Sister*. Anjelica Huston was the director, and the experience of working with her was its own true brush with greatness.

One day at lunch, Anjelica asked me about my name. She wanted to know what it was like having the name Bambi and working at Disney, so I told her my Michael Jackson story. To my surprise, she said she remembered that day well. She was playing opposite Michael as the wicked alien queen called the Supreme Leader in the *Captain EO* film. Anjelica said the reason that day stood out in her mind was the surprise visit from Elizabeth Taylor. Apparently Elizabeth wanted everyone to know that she was unhappy. It had something to do with her not being cast in the role opposite her friend Michael.

Thanks to Michael Jackson's childlike curiosity in wanting to meet the real live Bambi at Disney, I had one of my most remarkable brushes with greatness. In some ways, it set the benchmark for all others to come, and because of Michael Jackson, I no longer gave any further consideration to changing my name.

Chapter 5

Phone Home

Throughout the 1980s and '90s, Disneyland / Vista Records was the largest children's record label in the world. That distinction made it the desirable place for companies like Lucasfilm, owned by George Lucas at the time, and Steven Spielberg's Amblin Entertainment to license their family-oriented movies to Disney to develop, produce, and sell children's records based on their properties.

After releasing a successful line of products based on *Star Wars*, Disney Records head honcho Gary Krisel set his sights on *E.T.* Securing the rights to *E.T.* was a coup but posed a creative challenge in how to come up with a unique version of the story, since Michael Jackson had just recorded a version of his own.

Jymn Magon was my boss at the time and had the reputation for being a wunderkind. Jymn had authored more read-along scripts and had more gold and platinum albums than anyone else in the record business. Jymn wrote the script for *E.T. the Extra-Terrestrial as Told by Gertie*, and I was about to have a memorable *double* BWG.

Drew Barrymore was all of seven years old when she and her mother, Ildiko Jaid, turned up at the recording session. Drew played a character named Gertie in the film, and she was there to narrate the story of *E.T.* Drew was adorable and precocious and had one thing on her mind that day: how to get the grown-ups in the room to give her chocolate. In her mind, I did not qualify as a grown-up, which is something I could understand. I have always had a playful nature, and children have an innate sense of that. In truth, I was happy to participate when Drew enlisted my help to secure more chocolate for a share of the take. There was lots of giggling that day in the studio. In fact, I am especially grateful for the playful photo taken of Drew and me with her strategically placed "bunny ears."

Normally, Jymn would direct the recording session, but at the last minute, Steven Spielberg offered to do it. Watching Mr. Spielberg at work was thrilling. It was like attending a master class in direction. He began the recording session by having Drew repeat the lines back to him using a call-and-response technique. At first, Drew appeared to flub her lines, and Steven, quickly assessing her problem, took action. He said to Drew, "Remember the little man?" We watched from the booth as Steven took off his leather jacket and placed it on the floor next to the seat where Drew was sitting. Then he took off his boots and placed them at the base of the jacket. He laid a baseball cap on the floor by the collar of the jacket. Suddenly Drew's imaginary friend appeared, and according to Drew's mother, Mr. Spielberg had used this method to direct Drew during the filming of *E.T.* Drew sailed through the rest of the recording session. It was hard to believe that she was only seven at the time and such a talented professional. Everyone present that day felt lucky just to be in the room.

In my role as supervisor of product development, I was responsible for coordinating all approvals related to the production. This included all artwork, photos, and layouts, as well as audio tracks. In other words, I was a liaison between Disneyland / Vista Records and, in this case, Universal Studios and Steven Spielberg's Amblin Entertainment. Mr. Spielberg named his company Amblin after his first commercially released short independent film of the same name. His offices were located on the Universal Studios back lot. It was my job to go to the offices and secure the required signatures.

Let me digress for a minute. Remember, I was nearly born there and had a strong connection to Universal Studios. If one can claim that one's destiny might be preordained, then my becoming a tour guide at Universal surely comes close. When I was a college student, I landed one of the greatest summer jobs anyone could ever have. Where else could I share my anecdotal stories with a captive audience of up to 750 people each day? I felt so lucky being paid for doing something I loved. Becoming a Universal Studios tour guide is one of those seminal jobs like being a page at NBC or working in the mailroom at a talent agency. Getting one of these jobs could practically ensure a foot in the door to the entertainment industry. The training and testing process to become a tour guide was akin to going through boot camp. If you survived, you were hired.

Once you became a guide, you were encouraged to spend your days off at work. The studio bosses thought that the more you knew about the business, the better guide you would become. This meant free run of the back lot, which included visiting sets, watching filming, and going to the various departments involved in making movies and TV shows.

The education was priceless, and the brushes were the greatest. I loved Foley and special visual effects. I would spend hours watching the Foley artists making magic by adding sound effects to the visuals at hand. There were the footsteps of the Hardy Boys running down the street, or the sounds inside the spaceship on *Battlestar Galactica*, or the hustle and bustle of Cabot Cove as Jessica Fletcher (Angela Lansbury) entered a scene on *Murder She Wrote*. It was amazing to witness what these wizards would use, everything from an empty milk carton to a cat scratching post to a pair of coconuts banged together, to create the very real sound effects that we often take for granted.

I was equally interested in visual effects involving matte paintings. I jumped at the chance to watch Academy Award–winning Albert Whitlock and his matte department create paintings for the upcoming film *The Blues Brothers*, starring John Belushi and Dan Aykroyd.

One day, while on my way to their studio office, I turned the corner to go into the building and literally ran into Alfred Hitchcock as he was leaving. How many times had I passed the *Psycho* house, a favorite site on the studio tour, and talked about the brilliance of this great director—and suddenly there he was?!

Mr. Hitchcock was extremely reclusive, especially in his later years, and so a sighting like mine was extremely rare. Actually, what I remember about that moment was looking him squarely in the eyes and immediately turning away. He glared at me with a mean look on his face and, without uttering a single word, let me know that he was annoyed by the encounter.

Though it was only an impression and happened so quickly, it stayed with me for a long time. Sometimes a *disturbing* brush can appear to be larger-than-life, and this one certainly was.

Okay, so back to my *E.T.* story. I knew the Universal Studios lot like the back of my hand and literally got goose bumps every time I entered through the guard gates—especially as a young Disney Studio executive. As I mentioned earlier, part of my job was to acquire signatures for all approvals, and something critical happened on the *E.T.* project that could have cost me my job.

There are twenty-five pictures including the cover in the twenty-four-page book that accompanies the record. The photos selected came from approved photos from the film that the filmmakers provided to all their brand licensees. For example, Topps bubble gum had access to the same select photos for its bubble gum card collection featuring *E.T.* as Disney did. I secured the signatures from the Universal marketing rep and Steven Spielberg's office for the final layout before the books were printed.

Several weeks later, the books arrived. I knew something was up when I got called into my boss's office. He looked very upset. He called me over to his desk and opened the book to the last page. "What do you see?" he said. My mind was racing; was this a trick question? I paused and said, "It's E.T. holding the flowerpot Gertie

Drew Barrymore and me

gave him." I looked closer for signs of a bad printing job, and then I saw it. The photo revealed the wires they had used to operate E.T. Apparently no one had noticed this before, and now we had a full print run of books in our warehouse, and Universal and Amblin wanted them destroyed, which would delay our release and, well, cost somebody a lot of money or maybe even their job. I immediately said I didn't think it was our fault, because everyone had signed off on it. My boss looked at me and asked, "Do you have proof?" I said yes and showed him the signatures I got on the final layout. Talk about a Hail Mary that thankfully went my way.

The *E.T.* story record sold over a million copies, and one of my prized possessions is the gold record I received for my work on it.

My gold record for *E.T.*, commemorating one million in sales

Earlier, I described this as a double brush experience. It was not until years later, while on a flight coming home from New York, I saw Drew Barrymore again. I thought about approaching her.

Seeing Drew, age-wise now a grown-up herself, I wondered if she would remember that day in the recording studio so many years earlier. I decided to say hello, and I quickly recalled the occasion of

E.T. the Extra-Terrestrial as Told by Gertie record cover and disc

Steven Spielberg directing Drew Barrymore (later signed by Drew)

Yours truly in my Universal Studios tour guide uniform

our first meeting. Drew listened intently and smiled. Grasping my hand, she thanked me for the memory. She said she did not have too many of her own from that period in her life—at least not happy ones—and she appreciated my sharing mine with her. There was something so unexpected and heartbreaking about her response.

Sometimes we never know how our story can have an impact on someone else's life. My double brush with Drew was a genuinely bittersweet one.

Chapter 6

Sparky

The number one top-selling album in the world in 1983 was the movie soundtrack for *Flashdance*. *Flashdance* became part of our pop culture by influencing music, fashion, and art. Just about everyone I knew had torn the collars off their sweatshirts, signed up for a dance class, and sang along to Irene Cara's "Flashdance . . . What a Feeling." Irene Cara, the unknown actor who performed in the first musical I ever saw, *The Me Nobody Knows*, was now a pop sensation.

The Disneyland / Vista Records product development team considered any fad, trend, or craze a potential concept for song albums featuring the Disney core characters Mickey, Goofy, Donald, Minnie, and Daisy. The multiplatinum-selling Mickey Mouse disco album successfully thrust Mickey and friends into the contemporary spotlight.

Lee Mendelson, the multi–Emmy Award–winning producer of *Charlie Brown* and *Garfield*, knew this when he came up with the idea for his next *Peanuts* animated television special and called it *It's Flashbeagle, Charlie Brown*. He wanted Disneyland / Vista Records to put out an accompanying soundtrack. *Flashbeagle* the album was born.

Meeting Desirée Goyette and Ed Bogas, the talented music team responsible for all the music in the *Charlie Brown* specials, was serendipitous. Desirée is a multitalented musician and performer. Not only did she co-write the music and songs for numerous animated series, but she is also the voice of Betty Boop.

We hit it off from the moment we met and were fortunate enough to be able to work together and in some instances play together. Record promotion in the children's category is a lot different from contemporary music. It was unlikely that you would hear a song on the radio from a kid's record, and yet the production quality and musicianship were comparable. We often tried to think outside the box in finding ways to promote our new releases. For *Flashbeagle*, we decided to set up a tour around the country. Instead of concert halls, clubs, and restaurants, we played shopping malls. We went straight to the place where kids would gather, and Desirée and Snoopy would sing, dance, and put on a show. We drew crowds wherever we went and sold a lot of *Flashbeagle* merchandise too.

Everyone involved pulled out all the creative stops. Bill Meyers, best known for his work on Earth, Wind & Fire's hit "Let's Groove," did the horn arrangements on some of the songs. Lee Mendelson and his team decided to create an animated music video for the song "Pigpen Hoedown." In fact, Desirée, Jymn Magon, Bill Meyers, and I were rotoscoped into a dance sequence of the song. Rotoscoping is an animation technique used to trace over motion picture footage to produce realistic action. I was now officially an animated character.

My friendship with Desirée blossomed, and I felt honored when I was invited to her wedding. She married Lee at the Bel Air Hotel, and I wore a striking blue dress while posing for a picture with the groom.

Thanks to my friendship with Desirée and Lee, I was about to meet one of the greatest comic strip legends of all time and have a truly *animated* brush with greatness.

I grew up listening to the Royal Guardsmen's "Snoopy vs. the Red Baron" and reading the *Peanuts* comic strip. I had many Lucys in my life, so I always felt a sympathetic bond with Charlie Brown. Hearing the first piano notes of Vince Guaraldi's "Linus and Lucy" theme always made me want to get up and dance. It sounded like happy music to me. Each holiday season would start and end with the annual viewing of *It's the Great Pumpkin, Charlie Brown* and the classic *A Charlie Brown Christmas*. I always looked forward to finding a home for my own Charlie Brown Christmas tree.

I will never forget the day I met the man known to his friends as "Sparky." I was sitting alone in the inner sanctum of the Santa Rosa Ice Rink, home to Charles M. Schulz and his world of *Peanuts*. As I looked around the room while waiting to meet with Mr. Schulz, I saw that there were several drawings of *Peanuts* characters hanging on the walls. It struck me how the image of Snoopy, pictured ice-skating with reckless abandon, was the one I felt was closest to his creator. Mr. Schulz appeared to me to be a shy and unassuming man. He was extremely nice to me.

I remember someone telling me that he had applied for work as a Disney animator and did not get the job. Thank goodness, because we may never have had Snoopy to love.

I wrote to thank Mr. Schulz for his kindness and hospitality during our visit. I will always treasure the response I received from the man who created the world's most famous World War I beagle fighter pilot. On Mr. Schulz's stationery is the iconic drawing of Snoopy sitting on his doghouse at the typewriter. The letter was typewritten, except for Mr. Schulz's signature, which he signed "Sparky." Then, in his own hand, he drew a heart on the page as if emanating from the typewriter. What a beautiful, heartfelt brush with greatness!

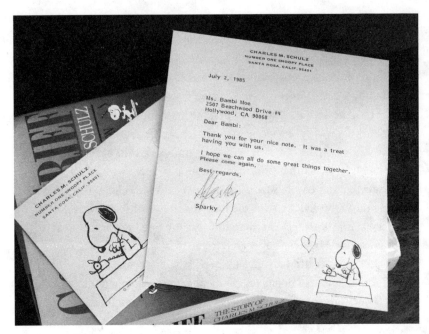

Note from Sparky

Me and Lee Mendelson

Me and Desirée

Chapter 7

The Disney Girls

John Braheny and Len Chandler founded the Los Angeles Songwriters Showcase (LASS) in 1971. A decade later, I became a regular attendee. The mission of the organization was to provide song critiques to material submitted by novice and veteran songwriters alike. There was no better way to network and establish contacts in the industry. Cassette Roulette and Pitch-A-Thon were two great resources for discovering new songwriters. John and Len also featured a Q&A with hit songwriters and industry leaders. I learned all about the craft of songwriting by attending LASS events. Part of my job as copyright assistant in Music Publishing was to look for potential songs and songwriters for Disney projects. It was at a Los Angeles Songwriters Showcase that I met Edwin Starr. I listened intently to what Mr. Starr said about songwriting and how he gave meaningful feedback to the writer of the song he had just heard. I realized in that moment that songs are like children to the songwriter, and art is subjective. I wish I could remember exactly what he said, but my gut told me that a man like Edwin Starr, who had numerous hits in his career, including the iconic song "War," might get a kick out of the idea of performing on a Disney record. I do remember approaching him and handing him my Disneyland / Vista Records business card with a gold-embossed Mickey Mouse on it. From this chance meeting, I had a fortuitous BWG with a music legend.

Following the success of *Mickey Mouse Disco*, *Mousercise* was Disney's parody answer to the fitness phenomenon popularized by Jane Fonda and others. I hoped my Disney bosses would be open to the idea of Edwin Starr's potential musical contribution. Edwin was so enthused and inspired by the idea that he arrived at the meeting with two song demos already in hand. The songs he wrote and recorded were "Get the Money (Uncle Scrooge's Money)" and "Tweedle Dee and Tweedle Dum." Both songs stood out because of their contemporary feel and the uniqueness of featuring lesser-known Disney characters in song. Thankfully, my bosses loved them.

Many things made my job fun. For example, during the promotion of the record, I got to Mousercise with exercise guru Richard Simmons on TV. I appeared on LA radio, Mousercising with DJs Bruce and Tony, who got a big kick out of meeting Bambi from Disney. After a brief interview, they played Beverly Bremers's *Mousercise* theme, including a Disney song medley set to a dance beat.

Mickey Mouse and friends had yet another award-winning platinum hit record, and it was the first Disneyland record made into a Disney Channel children's series.

Thanks to Edwin Starr's contribution, Beverly Bremers's *Mousercise* theme, and some good instincts on my part, I earned my first promotion. This truly was a *fortuitous* brush with greatness. I had learned the ins and outs of music publishing while working as a copyright assistant. The positive recognition of my work made me want to work even harder. I loved the variety of projects and the opportunity to wear many hats. It was under Jymn Magon's tutelage that I became supervisor of product development and learned how to produce storybooks and records, song albums, and music videos.

By the mid-eighties, I was working with the greatest character voice actors in the world: namely, Mickey Mouse, Donald Duck, and Goofy.

I will never forget my first encounter with Clarence "Ducky" Nash, the original voice of Donald Duck. Ducky was a bit of a rascal and flirt and not unlike the character he brought to life. He popped his head into my office with a quick "Hiya, Toots," and blew me a kiss.

I always thought that Donald Duck was the most difficult voice to imitate. Ducky not only created the sound of Donald but also was a tremendous actor, which helped to give Donald a personality possessing both heart and humor; this was Mr. Nash's legacy. Tony Anselmo, a young Disney animator, became Ducky's protégé and eventually took over voicing Donald Duck. However, in my opinion, no one, including Tony, ever rivaled Ducky's acting ability.

Goofy had a couple of voice actors in his life. Pinto Colvig was the original voice. I got to work with Bill Farmer, who embodied Goofy's humorous humanity. My early relationships with the actors voicing the Disney characters wound up being very important to me later on, especially once I started working for the Television Animation group. Bill Farmer and I worked on several projects together, including *A Goofy Movie* and *An Extremely Goofy Movie*, which you will hear more about later. With Bill, I always felt as if I was working with a treasured friend, albeit a Goofy one.

Mickey Mouse, on the other hand, had a résumé of voice actors to his name. Walt Disney gave Mickey his first voice, followed by Jimmy Macdonald. Pete Renaday, who worked in the Studio Music department, sometimes performed Mickey's voice. I worked with Wayne Allwine for most of my twenty years at Disney Studios. Wayne brought a cheerful innocence to his Mickey, and to be honest, Mickey's voice could sometimes come across like nails on a chalkboard. Yet Wayne always made sure that Mickey had a sense of humor. SPOILER ALERT: skip the next few sentences and read ahead if you're one of those people who don't want to suspend their disbelief. Mickey and Minnie were married—no, not the characters but the voice actors. Wayne married Russi Taylor, cast to voice Minnie Mouse. I am sure I was not the only one who wondered what a knock-down, drag-out fight and make-up session would sound like in that house.

Sadly, both Wayne and Russi have passed away, marking the end of an era and taking a bit of Mickey and Minnie with them. In my heart, I know they would have loved the Disney Legends memorial tributes from their animated pals, a testimony to the legacy of love they shared with the world.

Totally Minnie was the one project that stood out as the most near and dear to my heart. What made *Totally Minnie* so special was that, for the first time, the spotlight was to shine on the Disney girls: Minnie Mouse, Daisy Duck, Clarabelle Cow, and me.

As a fellow Disney girl, I felt a great responsibility to give Minnie, Daisy, and Clarabelle their ultimate musical coming-out party. In fact, I was involved in every aspect of the recording of *Totally Minnie*. I coproduced the album with Jai Winding, composer and music director for the Jackson 5 (which, if you recall, is one of the reasons why Michael Jackson wanted to meet me), and music executive Chris Montan. I introduced Pat DeRemer to the team, and he wrote, arranged, and sang on several songs for the album. Singer-songwriter Karla Bonoff sang "Dear Daisy," and Brenda Russell, who wrote and recorded numerous hit songs like "Piano in the Dark" and "Get Here" and years later cowrote the musical *The Color Purple*, sang the title track "Totally Minnie" and "Minnie's Workout." My friend Desirée Goyette sang the lead on the song "Hey Mickey," and if you listen closely, you might hear me singing in the chorus. "Oh, Mickey . . . you're so fine, you're so fine," our brush just blew my mind!

In the ongoing search for songs and songwriters, my next job assignment was to find new material for a band my Disney bosses were developing called Halyx. If the *Star Wars* cantina band were to mash up with Kiss and sprinkle in the playfulness of the Banana Splits, that could describe Halyx. A rock band that was literally out of this world, Halyx was amazing. As much as I loved finding songs for the Disney characters to sing, I found myself happily exploring a cool and hipper side of the music business.

"I Wanna Be Like M-O-U"

For *King Louie Swings In #4356-823*
Mark Jonathan Davis

LOUIE
Now I may be the king of the jungle
But around here I've been a fool
I dig the mouse
That gigs this house
I wish I could be so cool.

Oh, M.M., what's your secret?
How've you don't it all these years?
Tell me the scoop
Put me in the loop
Hey, Mi...

BG

we like you)

ey.

...havior
...d and comb my hair
...r sit upright
And be polite
And leave the jungle "out there."

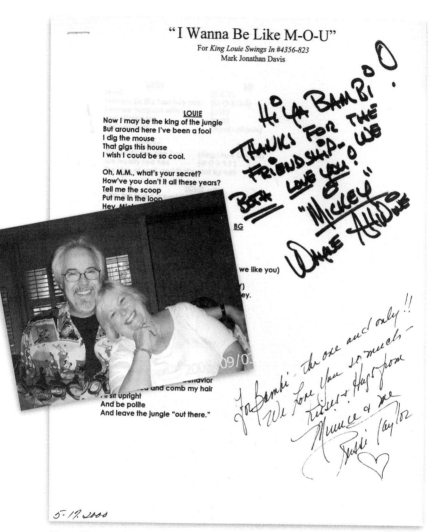

Wayne Allwine and Russi Taylor photo and note

Powerhouse lead singer Lora Mumford was the quintessential Princess Leia–style rocker chick, with Bruce Gowdy as her space-age boy-next-door lead guitarist. Master musician Roger Freeland was the band's seven-foot-tall Wookie-looking bass player, supported by Tony Coppola, a five-foot-tall, frog-like acrobatic percussionist. Rounding out the band was keyboardist Thom Miller, looking a lot like a storm trooper in his specially designed all-terrain vehicle, and Brian Lucas, the spaceman drummer on a rocket ship platform ready for liftoff. The future of Halyx looked promising in the hands of producer-composer Mike Post and Steve Geyer. The band signed with Elektra Asylum Records and built an audience while playing at the Disneyland Tomorrowland Terrace stage, and Halyx fans waited excitedly for the arrival of their debut album. Unfortunately, owing to corporate and executive changes at the label, the Halyx album never saw the light of day.

I cannot help but wonder what might have been, and apparently neither can independent-film director Matthew Serrano. Nearly forty years later, Halyx is the subject of a brand-new documentary by Serrano. Thanks to the internet, the popularity of this defunct band has developed a cultlike following. In a recent interview for the film, I told Matthew I could still remember the first time I heard Lora Mumford's haunting vocals on "Hey There Boys" and thinking, that is a hit song!

Thanks to Matthew and his team, I got a chance to reconnect with a few old friends like Roger Freeland and former Disney Records president Gary Krisel. They reminded me that I would always be a Disney girl at heart.

Brenda Russell, Minnie Mouse, Russell's manager Brenda Dash, and me

Chapter 8

Boxing Day

We were in the tiny English garden in the back of Julia Fordham's craftsman beach house in Santa Monica. Julia is a gifted singer-songwriter in her own right, and no matter how many times I hear her song "Girlfriend," it always makes me cry. As a Disney music executive, I became familiar with Julia's song catalog, and after meeting her, I hoped to find a Disney project for us to work on together. We instantly hit it off and became fast friends. Julia, in keeping with British holiday tradition, invited me to her Boxing Day party.

Allow me to set the scene: there were five of us sitting around a small, black wrought-iron table. The table was overflowing with beer and wine bottles and a half-dozen ashtrays packed with cigarette butts. The night air was cool. Candles illuminated the scene, dripping wax through the grating onto the ground. A woman named Gail sat to my right. Singer-songwriter Judith Owen sat across from me. Karen, Julia's next-door neighbor, sat next to her. Madame sat to my left.

She talks and smokes incessantly. She stands five foot six inches tall but acknowledges that most people think she is taller. Her mother was tall. She tried to look taller to please her. She overcame polio. She had it when she was nine. She said that if she didn't have polio, she would have been an athlete like her father. She described him as someone who was good with a stick and ball. She said that her father was especially disappointed that she waited until her twenty-second, or was it her twenty-third, album to dedicate it to him. It was the Mingus record and, arguably, her most controversial. She said Mingus wasn't crazy about it. She talked about how it made sense to dedicate that record to her parents, mainly because of the musical influences and collaborators who were of her parents' generation. I know she told us who, but I can't remember. She held court for several hours, four maybe. Trying desperately to soak it all in, I felt as if I had died and gone to heaven; and yet there I was, sharing an intimate evening's conversation with the goddess of all singer-songwriters: Joni Mitchell.

This had to be the ultimate experience of being at the right place at the right time. From a practical perspective, I thought I had better monitor my beer intake. There was no way I would vacate my "prime real estate" while sitting next to Joni, even if my bladder desperately called out for relief. The fact is, this was not my *first* brush with Madame.

Years earlier, when I was in my early twenties, I met a man named Jeffrey Husband. Jeffrey was the tour manager for the legendary rock band Crosby, Stills & Nash. Jeffrey lived his life on the road. Whenever Jeffrey made his way to Los Angeles, he called me. I must have seen CSN in concert more than a dozen times. On one occasion, Jeffrey invited me to a Graham Nash show at the Arlington Theatre in Santa Barbara. My best friend Jeanie Jefferds (daughter of Vince Jefferds) and I drove up early in the day so that we could get there between sound check and dinner. It turns out that Jackson Browne was Graham's special guest. When we got to the theatre, Jeffrey introduced us to Jackson and his pretty, willowy blonde girlfriend Daryl . . . as in Hannah. I had recently seen her in the Disney film *Splash*, in which she played a mermaid. This was way before *The Little Mermaid*, and I thought she was terrific. But I digress; my Joni Mitchell moment was completely unexpected, if not surreal.

During the concert, I sat onstage in the wings of this historic theatre. Instrument cartage crates were set between two thick, red velvet curtains. A woman approached with a lit cigarette in hand and sat down next to me. I was just about to blast her for smoking too close to the curtains when I saw out of the corner of my eye that it was Joni Mitchell. I could not believe it; I found myself distracted and equally appalled at the idea of a singer of her stature smoking. By keeping my mouth shut and not making a fuss, I had my own private Joni Mitchell concert. I held my breath as she sang along with Jackson and Graham while sitting next to me in the wings.

In that moment, while sitting in Julia Fordham's garden, I wondered if I should mention my previous brush with her. I decided not to. I did not want to break the spell of the evening's conversation. I wanted to recall as much of it as I could. The beauty of this brush lies in sharing what I heard that night.

Her sun sign is Scorpio. She read a book called *The Secret Language of Destiny*. She talked about her belief in what the book says about an individual's purpose in life. She likes to look up people she knows because it helps to give her compassionate insight. She has many Pisces, Capricorns, and Sagittarians in her life. She said a Dutchman and a Jew wrote the book. She is part French and described it as the impetus of her snobbery. She referred to herself as a loner but has a group of friends who gather every Sunday. She mentioned there is one individual who engages her in conversations that ultimately get combative. She looked up his birth chart in the book. She discovered a direct correlation between what she read about him in the book and her experience of him. She has since grown to appreciate and recognize his playful nature when he attempts to shift their intense dialogues into a lighter phase of conversation. Although she clearly cares about this person, she does not name him. However, she acknowledges that for the longest time, he drove her crazy.

She describes herself as a cat person and has two cats. However, Coco, her most lovable and uncharacteristically least hyperactive

Jack Russell terrier, calmly sat on her lap as Madame engaged us with her stories. Coco wore a brown sweater and a bejeweled collar. She said Coco was a year old. Her Sunday meeting friends suggested she get a dog. Actually, they stopped by a pet store, and she felt set up, as everyone in the store insisted that Coco was the dog for her. Reluctantly, she assumed responsibility for Coco, though she tried to return her twice, because she did not think she had what it took to be a good doggie caretaker.

Joni's daughter Kilauren was also at the party. I found out later that they were recently reunited. Joni had given her up for adoption at birth. Kilauren appeared to hover nearby, never straying far from her mother, and yet never engaging in our conversation. Kilauren is tall, maybe five nine or five ten. She was blonde like her mom, with exactly the same hair color, which glowed in the candlelight. She is willowy and has a husky voice. At some point, Madame got up from the table. I overheard someone ask Kilauren where her mother was. I suppressed a laugh when she said, "She's in the bathroom with my sister"—of course, referring to Coco the dog.

We began a group discussion about first loves. Madame said she was a good girl, though she was madly attracted to a hometown boy. She said his name, but I didn't quite hear it. It sounded like Southerland. She said they had shared feelings of real love between them. They would go out in his father's convertible to a point out by the airport, and they would sit and watch planes fly overhead. She said she wrote a song about him called "Ray's Dad's Cadillac." Maybe his first name was Ray, I thought. He was respectful of her, and she was a good girl . . . then. She said she lost him to her best friend Ariel. Ariel was a girl with a bit of a reputation and big boobs to boot. He wound up doing the right thing and married her to give her a good name. A couple of years ago, Madame, who is also a painter, had a gallery showing in her hometown, and it happened to coincide with her high school reunion. Anyway, there he was. She had not seen him in years, but she described him as a still-gorgeous farm boy with movie star good looks.

I noticed how she talks with her hands and always with cigarette tucked between her index and middle finger. She is right-handed, and I found myself dodging the tip of her cigarette as she was making a point about something.

Madame began telling us about her new album and recording it at AIR Lyndhurst Studios in London. She talked about the unusual tunings she uses on some of her songs. She thought it was interesting how they translated into orchestral arrangements. She spoke about the differences between electric and acoustic instruments, and I heard her say that to be truly creative, you cannot be afraid to fail.

The conversation shifted, and Joni began to tell a story about the Grammys. It was hard to believe, but she said the producers had never asked her to perform on the show. One year, however, when Prince was nominated for a Grammy, he specifically asked that Joni Mitchell present him with the award if he should win. She agreed to do it, but, of course, this meant that she needed to get a dress. It was all very last-minute, and a friend told her about a gorgeous white dress that had once belonged to Jennifer Jones and was in her size. Sight unseen, Madame had the dress sent over. Well, it was her size all right, but apparently Jennifer Jones is much taller than she is. There was nothing to do but try to belt up the dress with straps and ties. Her copresenting partner was Dionne Warwick. Madame chuckled while recounting how if you slow down the first few frames of picture, you could see Dionne's look of horror upon seeing the dress as she approached the podium. Madame described it as one of those moments you never forget.

As the evening wound down and we were all saying our goodbyes, Madame could not resist telling our host Julia one more story. She began by saying that she almost didn't make it to the party. Apparently, Joni Mitchell's ex-husband Larry Klein, who happened to be Julia's album producer, had completely forgotten that he had agreed to accompany her and her daughter to the gathering. When they got to his house, they found him at home, waiting for his date for the evening to arrive. She said she couldn't help but take a bit of

Julia Fordham

pleasure in watching him squirm. Larry did what any self-respecting
ex-husband of a superstar would do: he brought his date, his ex-wife,
and her long-lost daughter to the wonderful Boxing Day party.

To me, this was so much more than a "double" brush with greatness, when you encounter the same person more than once. Joni
Mitchell is part of my musical education. In my opinion, her words
and music exemplify a level of brilliance that remains peerless. The
storytelling aspects of her writing often influenced me in my work
at Disney. Listening to Joni Mitchell that evening was like attending
a priceless master class in artistry.

Graham Nash and me

Joni Mitchell

Chapter 9

Disney Diva and
The Little Mermaid (Ariel)

I left Disney in 1986 after five years at Disneyland / Vista Records. I felt it was time for me to spread my wings and fly into the real world. Having produced over sixty story records and song albums, I had achieved as much success as I thought possible then. MTV had burst onto the scene. I had just produced and edited the first animated music videos, "Hey Mickey" and "Totally Minnie," to air on the channel in regular rotation, which was a big deal at the time.

Who knows, if I had stayed, I might have remained a big fish in a little pond or, worse, become a Disney diva. In any case, I had nothing to worry about, because those invisible threads meant that Disney was never far from my life. As an independent contractor, I became an associate producer of the *Disney Sing-Along Songs* home video series. It helped that I knew where to find the animated footage with separate music and sound effects tracks. I worked as a production manager on the USA network series *The Hollywood Insider*, and I had the most fun working at Rhino Records.

I could probably write an entire book about my experiences at Rhino. My title was Director of Development and Production of Rhino Video. Unlike at Disney, which had layers and levels of approvals and bureaucracy, my beloved boss Richard Foos told me I could produce anything I wanted to as long as it didn't cost too much. Accepting the challenge, I put out a collection of animated short films in the public domain and called it *Weird Cartoons*, featuring the cult classic *Bambi Meets Godzilla* (I kept costs down, but we had to pay to license that one from creator Marv Newland). I also produced *Heart and Soul: The Official Monkee Videography* and had incredible brushes with Micky, Davy, Mike, and Peter. We sold a whopping twenty-five thousand units.

My Disney destiny collided when I literally ran into Gary Krisel, my former boss at Disneyland / Vista Records. Gary's career had skyrocketed, and he was now president of Walt Disney Television Animation (WDTVA). He invited me to lunch, asked what I had been up to, and said he had been looking for me. He told me that the Disney feature film *The Little Mermaid* had been so successful that he had been given the directive to develop and produce a half-hour television series featuring Disney's newest princess, Ariel, and her friends Sebastian the crab and fish sidekick Flounder. "We want to feature a new song in every episode, and I need someone who knows the craft of songwriting." Well, that was all I needed to hear; I said, "Sign me up."

The Little Mermaid was the first animated television series I ever worked on. Under Gary's leadership, WDTVA had become a very profitable division at The Walt Disney Company. Frankly, there was a bit of a rivalry between the Feature Animation group and us. However, and to their credit, Peter Schneider, Tom Schumacher, and the team at Walt Disney Feature Animation really put the animated musical feature film back on the map. Audiences loved Ariel and her friends, and we needed to make sure the television series maintained and grew the legacy.

When I returned to Disney on February 9, 1991, my new title was Associate Producer, Music, at WDTVA. My first task was to find a composer for *The Little Mermaid* TV series and begin developing ideas for a main title. Since Howard Ashman and Alan Menken, the composing talent from the feature film, were unavailable, I put out the word to the music community. I was reviewing demo tapes from music composers and songwriters for the project.

Inundated with demo tapes, I wound up developing a library of music talent. However, I noticed something odd and puzzling: a large number of demos came from various composers claiming to have worked on the Warner Bros. animated series *Tiny Toon Adventures*. I wondered how that was possible.

What I learned is how labor-intensive animated music composing is. For example, a single twenty-one-minute episode could include wall-to-wall music cues, written by four or five different composers, with one composer being responsible as the supervising composer. Because of the creative demands of writing that much music in a short period of time, multiple composers are brought in to assist; that's why Bruce Broughton, supervising composer of *Tiny Toon Adventures*, gave so many other composers a chance to work on the show.

When it came time to hire a *Little Mermaid* composer, our series director Jamie Mitchell chose Dan Foliart, who had won several Emmy Awards for composing music for TV series like *Home Improvement* and *Roseanne*. Our next step was to establish a main title theme for the series. After great debate, it was decided that it would be an instrumental medley of the themes from the movie—a little bit of "Under the Sea," "Part of Your World," and "Kiss the Girl."

With Dan Foliart in place, we recorded the main title and scored the first episode. By the time we started work on the second episode, our director Jamie Mitchell decided to go in a "different direction," and Dan left the project.

I immediately turned to my pile of demo tapes and remembered one in particular from a *Tiny Toon Adventures* composer named Mark Watters. Mark stood out from the rest because he had a gift for making a small group of musicians sound like an orchestra. Mark's skill for arranging and composing was economical, time-saving, and creative.

Once hired, Mark remained for the duration of the series. He skillfully created a musical library for Ariel and her underwater world.

During my Disney tenure, Mark Watters scored numerous series for which he deservingly won several Daytime Emmy Awards for his composition work. I had an Emmy Award BWG in 1995 when Mark, unable to attend the ceremony, asked me to accept the award on his behalf in the event of a win for the *Aladdin* TV series. My mother was able to attend the show as my guest, and she beamed with pride as I went onstage to accept the award. She told me later that it was her favorite brush with greatness.

My next challenge was to produce a song for each episode that would satisfy an army of corporate bosses as well as the director and writers of the series. Since music was a key ingredient to the success of the animated feature film, there was a company-wide high expectation for our TV show.

The process of producing the songs involved reading the script, meeting with the director and writers, and discussing if and where a song would work in each episode. I would then cast the appropriate songwriter and work with him or her on the demo. Once the demo was approved, I would send it to the talent.

The good news was that the original voice talent was available, including Jodi Benson, the embodiment of Princess Ariel. Like composers Howard Ashman and Alan Menken, Jodi Benson came from a Broadway talent pool. Jodi's sweet, innocent, yet strong voice captured the hearts of young girls all over the world while catapulting her to Disney Princess icon status. I went to see Jodi on Broadway when she landed the lead in the show *Crazy for You*, based on the music of George and Ira Gershwin. I thought she was terrific, but for me, nothing could compare to watching her in the studio, as she would close her eyes and suddenly become Ariel. It was important for us to protect and preserve Ariel's character and maintain the quality of Jodi's voice. With engineer James Twomey at the helm, we would usually record her vocals on Mondays, when most Broadway theatres are closed, giving Jodi time to rest her voice.

I mentioned earlier that, on a school trip to see a Broadway show, I had seen *Over Here!*, starring the Andrews Sisters. The talented cast included a number of notable names, including Sam Wright. This was another one of those invisible threads. Sam, a popular Broadway performer, provided the voice for Sebastian the crab. When I told Sam that I had seen him in *Over Here!*, he responded as if he barely remembered doing the show.

Scheduling Sam's voice sessions was often challenging because he lived two hours outside New York City. Sam would use the time in the limousine ride to hear the song—often for the very first time! Of course, this made the recording sessions a bit more difficult, because they took longer, as he would need time to learn the part and get into the character.

We recorded dozens of songs for *The Little Mermaid* TV series. Many of our WDTVA songs provided synergistic opportunities in other areas of the Disney Company. They wound up released on Walt Disney Records or appeared on a Disney Sing-Along Songs home video. I was especially proud to have come full circle and thrived in my new creative role at TV Animation. In a way, my leaving Disney and returning afforded me the opportunity to grow both personally and professionally.

One of my personal favorite *Little Mermaid* songs was written for a character called the Evil Manta. Tim Curry was set to voice the character. I loved *The Rocky Horror Picture Show*, and I had no idea what to expect when Mr. Curry came to the studio to record his vocals. Tim Curry's deep and menacing voice oozes with villainy, but his sexy and provocative portrayal of the flamboyant Dr. Frank-N-Furter left an indelible imprint in my mind. Imagine my surprise when I met Mr. Curry for the first time and found a reserved yet friendly, very kind, and thoughtful man—completely unlike any of the characters he had portrayed. For this reason, he was my most *surprising* brush with greatness.

I also loved working with Pat Carroll, our Ursula the sea witch. She was a joy to record and had a larger-than-life personality. Pat

Jodi Benson and me

Jodi Benson note

captured our hearts with her warm and billowy laugh that could fill a room, and I always sensed that she seemed genuinely grateful for every working opportunity. We had such a good time recording her song "You Wouldn't Want to Mess with Me," written by the gifted and prolific songwriting team of Kevin Quinn and Randy Petersen.

The idea of developing a series from a feature film proved extremely profitable to the Disney Company. *The Little Mermaid* TV series became a major hit in its own right, and from this point

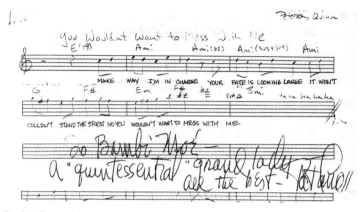

Pat Carroll song sheet

forward, synergy had become a creative driving force within the Disney Company.

There was something so magical about my return to Disney and having my first Disney Princess brushes with greatness. Thanks to Ariel and her friends, I was reminded how much I loved being part of that world.

Chapter 10

Beauty and the Beast (Belle)

With the arrival of *Beauty and the Beast* in 1991, the release of a Disney animated feature film became a highly anticipated event and provided unlimited synergistic opportunities.

Starting with *The Little Mermaid*, Broadway's hit composing team of Alan Menken and Howard Ashman had established their position as Disney music royalty. Beyond *Beauty and the Beast*, they were already hard at work on *Aladdin* when Howard Ashman became ill with AIDS. To me, the music for *Beauty and the Beast* is sheer perfection. The melodies are as catchy as one could imagine, and the lyrical brilliance magically sweeps the audience into the story right from the start. Howard Ashman's genius took the film to another level and would forever change the way we experience animated movies.

WDTVA began to develop ideas on how to create a franchise for Belle and her family of inanimate objects that came to life. We decided early on that there would be no TV series. Instead we would develop a long-form concept: a direct-to-video movie. This meant that we would have more time and music budget for *Beauty and the Beast: The Enchanted Christmas*, or at least I hoped so.

Not only was the original film a major box office success, but it was also lauded as creatively brilliant. Our direct-to-video movie was not really a sequel but a "mid-quell," because it tells the story of what happened during Christmastime, when the Beast held Belle captive. The stakes were high, and our musical casting choices would be under even greater scrutiny. I really struggled with what we could do musically and who could we get to make our project successful.

I searched the Broadway and off-Broadway musical theatre community to see if there were any writers up to the task. Unfortunately, my Feature Animation colleagues had already mined those fields. In fact, the pop music world was also off-limits, as Feature Animation was spending considerable amounts of money to attract major talent like Elton John and Phil Collins.

During this time, I also began working on *A Goofy Movie*, my first animated feature film. Disney artist Kevin Lima would be making his directorial debut. Kevin would become my first *colleague* BWG as the future director of *Tarzan*, and the mega box office hit film *Enchanted*.

Kevin had a short list of composers he wanted to score his film; among them was the name Rachel Portman. I loved her work, having seen the quirky romantic comedy *Benny and Joon*, starring Johnny Depp and Mary Stuart Masterson. Rachel's agent Richard Kraft set up a meeting in a New York recording studio where she was working so that I could show her a rough cut of *A Goofy Movie*.

Meeting a composer of Rachel's talent was the ultimate brush experience. I watched her as she watched the film, and I was relieved to see that she seemed to enjoy it, laughing in all the right places. When it ended, Rachel turned to me and said in a British accent, "It's lovely, but I prefer a blank canvas." I had no idea what she meant at first. I had just shown her an animated movie, so how could it be blank? Rachel explained that she would like to score an animated film, but she wanted to write the songs as well. The songs for *A Goofy Movie*, written by Grammy Award–winning songwriter Tom Snow and New York lyricist Jack Feldman, were already complete and recorded. It was clear that Rachel would not be scoring *A Goofy Movie*. However, intrigued by her interest in writing songs, I asked if she had ever written any songs before. She said no but she knew she could. I thought it would be great if I could find the right project for her. I went home and started listening to her scores and realized that a number of her cues sounded like unformed song melodies. Rachel's music is distinctive and whimsical.

I had an idea: what if I paired Rachel Portman with a veteran musical theatre lyricist? Maybe that could be the magic team to tackle *Beauty and the Beast: The Enchanted Christmas.* I pitched my plan to Gary Krisel, and he said "absolutely NO! Are you kidding? She has never written a song. This is too important a project to take that kind of a risk." I was devastated but determined.

With my idea shot down, I decided to look to the London theatre world for possible candidates. I spent a week meeting with virtually every songwriter in the UK. I could not shake the thought of pairing Rachel up with a lyricist.

My final meeting for the week was on Friday afternoon, and it turned out to be a *bonus* BWG. Having saved the best for last, I was about to meet one of my favorite songwriters, the lyricist Sir Don Black, who wrote the song "To Sir, with Love." As a teen, I had literally worn down the needle on my record player listening to Lulu's version repeatedly as I sang along. "To Sir, with Love" was the basis of the movie with the same name starring Sidney Poitier—a truly seminal song from a seminal movie.

Classy and elegant are two words that come to mind in describing Sir Don Black. I liked him instantly and felt immediately comfortable enough to share my wild idea with him. Much to my amazement, Don told me that he was a great fan of Rachel's work and he would love to meet her. Before leaving London, I arranged a meeting between the two. I was thrilled when they called me to say that they would absolutely love to work together and hoped it would be with me. Suddenly my dream team became a reality. How would I convince my boss, who had said "NO!" to my idea even after I begged him, and said he could fire me if I was wrong about my casting instincts?

Within a week after I returned home from my UK trip, Gary Krisel had left The Walt Disney Company. Dean Valentine became my new boss, and he gave me the okay to hire my dream team. However, my creative casting idea was once again nearly derailed by another twist of fate.

Before Rachel and Don could get started writing the songs for *Beauty and the Beast: The Enchanted Christmas*, Rachel Portman won an Academy Award for her film score to *Emma*. Practically overnight, she became the most sought-after composer in Hollywood. Her new ranking made her the first woman to win an Oscar for best original score. Rachel's commitment to our project and me was suddenly on shaky ground. Much to her agent's chagrin, Rachel honored her promise to me, and the resulting songs she wrote with Sir Don Black are wonderful little gems. Even the original cast said the songs were a delight to sing. In fact, Rachel and Don's signature song "As Long as There's Christmas" appears twice in the film, sung beautifully by Paige O'Hara, who played Belle, and the cast and again as the end title duet, sung by Grammy Award–winning artists Roberta Flack and Peabo Bryson.

Several of the voice actors and singers were based in New York and working on Broadway, so I flew there often to record. An unexpected encounter occurred while I was waiting for my baggage at JFK Airport. I saw Sidney Poitier standing by the baggage carousel and immediately thought what a great omen it was. I knew that Mr. Poitier held a seat on The Walt Disney Company board of directors, so as a fellow "cast member," I felt that it somehow made him accessible to me. With that in mind, I fearlessly decided to approach him. For a moment, I wondered if he knew about our *Beauty and the Beast* project. As I held out my hand and said my name, he quickly responded by saying, "I know who you are." I think my jaw dropped open, but no words came out. Finally, I spoke and asked, "Really, but how?" He warmly shook my hand and said that as a Disney board member, he had recently seen my name as part of an executive compensation review. Wow, I could not believe it. He asked me about my name. I told him the story I had told many times before, and then I happily relayed our Don Black connection. We talked for several minutes, and he mentioned that he had just seen Disney's *Aida* on Broadway. He said he especially loved Heather Headley's performance. I agreed and told him that she was my dear friend. We both marveled at the possibility that her recent Tony Award nomination could deservingly lead to a win for her star-making performance. I could not wait to share my Sidney Poitier brush with Don and Heather. The combined experience was like having a Super Bowl brush with greatness!

As my work on *Beauty and the Beast* continued, I could not have imagined that my next BWG with Tony, Oscar, Emmy, and BAFTA Award–winning performer Angela Lansbury would be so challenging. I was so excited about the prospect of working with this living legend that I could not have anticipated the difficulty we would encounter trying to get the vocal performance we needed.

A click track sounds like an audible metronome, and animators use it to lock in the timing of the voice in the animation. Angela Lansbury as Mrs. Potts had a couple of lines to sing, called a "step out." When Ms. Lansbury put on her headphones, what she heard was a "temp," or temporary music track, with click and along with all the other vocals.

The notion of recording to a prerecorded music track was foreign to her. She explained that when she had recorded the original songs from the first film, it was with a live orchestra, and they would follow her vocal. Our click track kept throwing her off, and yet without it, we could not lock in the vocal and ensure that the lip movement for her character would synchronize. What a predicament to be in with one of your heroes! If I could have produced an instant orchestra, I would have. Ms. Lansbury, being the pro that she was, was determined to work at it until we got it right. She came through! Nevertheless, it was my *most stressful* BWG.

Jerry Orbach, who played the role of Lumiere, arrived at the studio with his wife in tow. "Okay, let's get this over with. I'm in a hurry," he said. I smiled, thinking he was kidding. He was not. He had a driver waiting outside with the meter running. Not the most pleasant, but it was the fastest vocal performance I have ever recorded. Amazed though I was, Mr. Orbach stopped to pose for a picture.

If there is a *Guinness Book of World Records* category for producing song vocals with the greatest number of Tony Award–winning best actress musical performers, I think my name would be near the top of the list. To date, I have produced vocals with seven Broadway superstars.

I wept when I saw Bernadette Peters play opposite Mandy Patinkin in *Sunday in the Park with George*. She is one of Broadway's greatest performers, and having the chance to work with her would be a dream come true. When I heard that Ms. Peters had agreed to play a role in *Beauty and the Beast: The Enchanted Christmas*, I nearly fainted. The one thing that stood out in my mind about this particular brush was how petite and frail I thought Ms. Peters looked. An unimposing person with porcelain skin, runny nose, and tissue in hand . . . I marveled at how she pulled a powerfully emotional performance out of thin air. She was the perfect Christmas Angel.

In the end, any concern about how the music for *Beauty and the Beast: The Enchanted Christmas* would stand up on its own abated when Rachel Portman and Sir Don Black earned an Annie Award nomination for outstanding individual achievement for music in an animated feature production.

My personal passion for this project was so strong and deep that for the first time, having put my career on the line, I found myself staring into the mirror of my own creative soul. I am grateful to have had the opportunity to wholeheartedly pursue my dream and, in reality, brush up against true greatness.

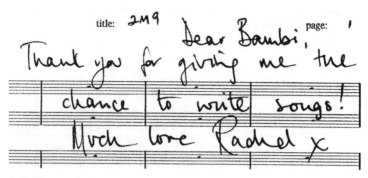

Rachel Portman thank-you note

DON BLACK

Rachel Portman, Sir Don Black, and me

As Long As There's Christmas (Reprise)

Bernadette Peters and me

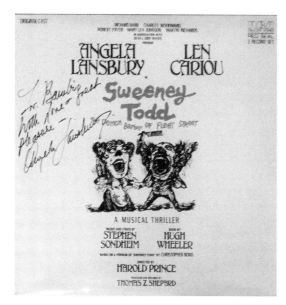

Angela Lansbury autograph

Jerry Orbach and me

Chapter 11

Hercules (Megara)

The premiere party for Disney's *Hercules* was quite a spectacle. It included a screening at the newly renovated New Amsterdam Theatre, a parade down Forty-Second Street, and an after-party on Chelsea Piers.

By the time I arrived at the after-party, Michael Bolton was singing a song from the film. Sharing the stage with the veteran vocalist was a petite powerhouse singer named Susan Egan. Susan was Disney's newest princess. She had already established a following as Belle on Broadway in *Beauty and the Beast* and was now the sultry voice of Megara, Hercules's love interest in the film. Our paths were destined to cross, but not on that night. Instead that night was all about meeting the voice of Hercules, Tate Donovan.

Tate had just signed on to do the sixty-five-episode animated series, and we would be working together. There is something so sweet about him, in a boy-next-door kind of way. I should not have been at all surprised when he introduced me to his girlfriend. She smiled and held out her hand. "Hi, I'm Jennifer," she said. Startled and instantly greeted by the warm, friendly smile on the face of TV's most popular girl next door, Jennifer Aniston, I awkwardly nodded and said, "Yes, I know who you are, and I'm a fan of your show." Sometimes brushes can catch you off guard, and this one certainly did.

I have run into Tate Donovan many times over the years, and he is always very down to earth. He went on to star opposite Glenn Close in the highly acclaimed series *Damages*. We recently met again, this time on the red carpet at the Emmy Awards. Tate was escorting his mom, who was his date that night, through the sea of cameras. He stopped for a moment to take a picture of her in front of an Emmy statue. I said hello and offered to take the picture of the two of them together. He thanked me. He said it was nice to see a friendly face in the crowd.

In addition to Tate Donovan, *Hercules* had a wonderful cast of voice actors and some of Broadway's greatest singers. Our singing Muses featured Lillias White, LaChanze, Roz Ryan, and Cheryl Freedman. Getting to work with them and hearing them sing was like going to church—a religious BWG experience.

The first time I saw Lillias White was in the 1987 revival of *Dream Girls*. She played Effie, and I remember she got a standing ovation that night. Ten years later, in 1997, Lillias won a Tony Award for best actress in a musical for her role in *The Life*. LaChanze was nominated for a Tony for her role in *Once on This Island* in 1991, but it wasn't until 2006 and her powerful performance in *The Color Purple* that she took home the statue. What a privilege it was to produce music with these women. It should not be at all surprising that our recording sessions were raucous, filled with laughter and joy.

The voice actors in *Hercules* included James Woods, French Stewart, Sandra Bernhard, Bobcat Goldthwait, Paul Shaffer, and Eric Idle. Working with performers who are not really singers made my job more interesting!

Directing nonsingers to sing is mostly about putting the artists at ease and helping them to get out of their own way. They each know the placement of their character's speaking voice, so the singing needs to be "less perfect" and more reflective of how that character would sound if he or she were to sing.

James Woods voiced the evil but humorous Hades, and he delivered his song vocal in the style of Rex Harrison, with kind of a talk-singing approach. French Stewart's character had a nervous, prepubescent, high-pitched voice, so we were never trying to capture a pleasant sound; in fact, the more imperfect, the better and funnier. The same was true for Sandra Bernhard and Bobcat Goldthwait, and in each case, I tried to get them to give me less, because the less over-the-top, the more believable the performance. My experience of working with Paul Shaffer and Eric Idle was unique because each of them wrote a song for their characters to sing.

Sometimes time constraints and talent availability required us to record in two different cities at the same time using ISDN phone lines. For example, I would be in a recording studio in Los Angeles, and the talent was in a studio in New York. Two engineers would coordinate the recording process by digitally broadcasting through telephone lines. Because of his commitment as the bandleader on *Late Night with David Letterman*, we had to record Paul Shaffer's song this way. The same was true for our recording with Susan Egan, who was starring on Broadway.

Susan is one of those rare performers who can make the work look easy. I had gone to see her at a Sunday matinee performance of *Beauty and the Beast* on Broadway. Susan, nominated for her role as Belle in the production, had quite a following. The mostly preadolescent crowd was so noisy that I could barely hear the dialogue, but Susan's performance was captivating. I intended to go backstage and introduce myself. I thought better of it when I caught a glimpse of the long line of little girls enthusiastically waiting for their Belle to emerge and hoping for an autograph. This brush was not meant to be, or at least not at this particular time.

The series writer-creators of Disney's *Hercules* were big Susan Egan fans. Unfortunately, the series is set during the time when young Hercules is in high school, long before he meets Susan's character and future love interest, Megara. To Susan's credit and talent, the writers were committed to writing Meg into a "special" episode, and I knew they would want to make the most out of it and have her sing.

Songwriters Randy Petersen and Kevin Quinn came up with a terrific song for Meg called "The Man That I Love," but owing to time constraints and the fact that Susan was starring on Broadway, I could not get to New York in time to record the song, so we recorded via ISDN. Working coast to coast, we immediately connected. Susan was so well prepared that she needed little or no direction. The song came out great, and we both said how much we looked forward to the day we would get to meet in person.

Our face-to-face meeting happened backstage at Studio 54. Susan was starring as Sally Bowles in the Broadway revival of *Cabaret* with her costar Michael C. Hall (*Dexter* and *Six Feet Under*) as the Emcee. Our bond was immediate and long-lasting. From that point on, our paths continued to cross. We worked together again on *Lady and the Tramp II: Scamp's Adventure*, as well as a number of other recording projects. Sometimes a brush with greatness is well worth the wait and can turn into a lifelong friendship, as it has with Susan.

My first encounter with Eric Idle began on the phone. We started talking about his character Prometheus, and he told me he had an idea for a song. I knew that a song written and performed by Eric would be a great addition to the *Hercules* TV series. After all, anyone familiar with the brilliant humor of Monty Python and their classic silly songs like "The Lumberjack Song" and the Eric Idle–penned "Always Look on the Bright Side of Life" would have to agree!

I remember my surprise when Eric said he had not written a song in quite a while and did not have the means available to record a song demo. I told him it was not a problem, and I knew just what to do. I called Randy Petersen, one of my favorite songwriters, and asked him if he would help Eric out. He did, and by the time we got to the session to record the "Promethean Ditty," it was clear that we had one heck of a silly song. In addition, if a picture paints a thousand words, then you can tell I had one of my funniest BWGs, all thanks to Eric Idle.

From a musical perspective, *Hercules* proved to be one of the most exciting shows I have ever music supervised. We recorded more songs in *Hercules* than in any other animated TV series. I worked with great singers and nonsingers alike and had the privilege of discovering a gifted composer by the name of Adam Berry.

Hiring a composer for a series is a lot like casting actors; you want to find the right person for the job. The *Hercules* series creators really wanted me to find a fresh, new music talent. Having heard Adam's music on a couple of episodes of *South Park*, I was convinced that he had that special creative quality we were looking for.

The demands on the composer for an animated series are extremely intense. The episodes "spotted" on a Monday with nearly twenty-one minutes of wall-to-wall music recorded by Friday. Spotting is the process of watching the show with the "creatives"; this usually includes the director, writer, editor, composer, and me. Depending on the director's approach, the scenes are broken down and discussed in terms of mood, feel, tempo, and even color. Often a composers' job is to play up the humor in a scene. Adam Berry had a natural instinct and always knew what to do. He is a multitalented musician. Adam is also the recipient of both an Emmy Award for Outstanding Music Direction and Composition and a Grammy Award for Best New Age Album with his group White Sun.

The *Hercules* series, rich in singing talent, gave me the opportunity to produce a song with Idina Menzel. I had just seen *Rent* on Broadway and loved the show. The extraordinarily talented cast included Idina and her boyfriend at the time, Taye Diggs. Disney's Hollywood Records had just signed Idina to a recording deal, and I really championed recording a song with her for *Hercules*. I pitched the synergistic idea to the series writers, and they came up with the character of Circe. I commissioned a song and hoped that Idina would like it and that the Hollywood Records executives would approve.

Meeting Idina and working with her was a doubly charged encounter. I was already a fan, and I wanted to like her. Obviously, liking someone is not critical to working together, but it definitely

Tate Donovan and me

Idina Menzel and me

Paul Shaffer

Susan Egan on the cover of *In Theater*, October 4, 1999

helps. Thankfully, I was not disappointed; what a warm, wonderful, and gifted talent she is. It turns out that we both grew up on Long Island, which for me explains her naturally funny and down-to-earth personality.

I had just finished the recording session with Idina when in walked Taye Diggs. Be still my heart, what a smile that man has! At the time, Taye and Idina were dating; they later married and divorced. Idina had left before Taye arrived, and I was racing out to get to another meeting and unsure of how to get there. Taye graciously offered to escort me. He also did not mind me asking him to sign my copy of the libretto for *Rent*, which I had with me. He wrote, "Bambi baby what can I say! You seem very nice—I'm sure it's the case. Peace and Blessings Taye Diggs." Meeting Taye Diggs was a wonderful and *unexpected* BWG.

Idina would go on to win a Tony Award for Best Actress in a musical for her role in *Wicked*. She has also become a Disney

Eric Idle and me

Susan Egan and me

Rent libretto pages for Idina Menzel and Taye Diggs

Adam Berry and me

superstar, especially in the eyes of little boys and girls all over the globe, for her role as Elsa in *Frozen* and her performance of the Oscar-winning song "Let It Go."

We recently had a *double* brush. I went backstage to say hello to Idina after her performance in a play called *If/Then* at the Pantages Theatre. Receiving a warm greeting, I congratulated her on her recent marriage to Aaron Lohr and asked her to say hello to him for me. She was puzzled by the connection, and I explained that Aaron and I had worked together when he sang the vocals as Goofy's son Max in *A Goofy Movie*.

I guess it really is a small world after all.

Chapter 12

Beth

When you get a call from Thom Rollerson of the Dream Foundation, it always means two things: first, he wants something; and second, you are going to give it to him. Ordinarily this might seem a bit obnoxious, but Thom's heart is always in the right place, and you know that his call is a chance to do some good. Besides, Thom embraced me as an extended member of the Jefferds family; his brother Jimmy had married my best friend Jeanie's younger sister Jenny. Thom knew I held an executive position in music at The Walt Disney Company.

The Dream Foundation is the only national nonprofit organization devoted to granting the last wish of terminally ill adults. The day Thom called me, he said, "I have a dream recipient that I want you to meet. Her name is Elizabeth Rorman. Beth's dream has to do with how music has affected her life and her family. She wants to tell her story. Do you think you can find a cameraman and go interview her and film it?" Without hesitation, I said, "Yes."

I immediately thought of my dear friend Basem Wasef, a colleague who worked at the Disney Channel. He was branching out in his career and filming commercials. I called him and told him what I knew about Beth: she was the mother of two boys, Joshua and Ben; a wife to Michael; and the daughter of Clara. I took a deep breath and said, "Beth is dying of cancer." Basem's response was "Tell me what I can do?" and I said, "Bring your camera and take this journey with me."

We arrived at the Rorman home, and to be honest, I was extremely nervous. I had no idea what we were getting into. Beth greeted us warmly at the door, and it was clear that the ravages of this despicable disease had taken its toll on her. Something extraordinary happened that day as we fumbled our way through the interview. I confessed to Beth that I had never done anything like this before, and I wanted it to be a great experience for her. Her smile gave me comfort, as if she already knew I would not let her down.

Sitting across from this woman warrior, I listened to her tell her story of meeting and marrying Michael, her high school sweetheart, and about the births of her beloved boys. She spoke of the love and gratitude for her mom, Clara, who quit her job so that she could selflessly take care of her daughter. In that moment, I knew that knowing Beth would change my life forever.

She had an indescribable inner strength that allowed her to open up and reveal her soul to me, a complete stranger. Beth shared the details of her treatment, including the long weekly sojourns to the City of Hope. The two-and-a-half-hour drive each way by car with Mike and the boys was spent listening to and singing along with their favorite recording artist Celine Dion. Beth lit up as she talked about her love of Celine's voice, describing the way Dion interpreted the lyrics to her songs and how everyone in the family had their favorite tracks. "Play number 8! No, stop . . . play 5!" as they would lovingly argue over which songs to play first.

At one point, Beth acknowledged it was her dream to meet Celine Dion, to share the experience with her family, to give to them a memory to cherish long after she passed. Beth told me that someone had recently asked her if, given the choice of having cancer or not, what would she choose? Beth said that the question gave her pause, because as much as she wouldn't want to have the cancer, she also knew that she would not have experienced the gift of knowing all the people who had come into her life, and she wasn't sure she could give that up. I could no longer keep my composure, and my eyes flooded with tears.

We finished our filming. Basem and I began the editing process. I felt guided by the music choices that accompanied Beth's story. We were working against time, and it meant so much to be able to share the film with Beth. Nevertheless, what Beth didn't know was that the kind and caring folks at the Dream Foundation were using all their contacts to reach out to Celine Dion. They had hoped to send Beth and her family to Las Vegas to meet Celine and attend her show.

Each day seemed to carry an added weight as we waited to hear from Celine's camp. We were told that they get hundreds of requests like this every month. With our film nearing completion, I knew we had done our best to capture the radiant essence of Beth in her own words.

Then the news came that the meeting with Celine would happen. Beth told me she was over the moon, and everyone was giddy with excitement, but there was real concern about whether or not Beth was physically up to it. One of the conditions of the meeting held the restriction that we could not film or publicize it in any way. My hope was that an exception could be made, thereby allowing us to capture the moment. Thom suggested I write a personal letter to Celine and send along a copy of our unfinished film. I explained in my letter that allowing us to document the meeting on film would be the best way to honor Beth's dream and her desire to give her family a shared and lasting memory. I also said that I would understand if they said no, but I had hoped Celine would look at the film and get a sense of the extraordinary woman she had generously agreed to meet.

Again we waited, and as the day approached for the Rormans to leave for Las Vegas, I went to visit Beth. She assumed that Basem and I were going with them. I explained that there was a restriction, and we were not going. Promising to be there in spirit, I told Beth I could not wait to hear all about their adventure. Over the course of several weeks, I had become an extended family member and now felt crushed at the thought of missing the experience of seeing Beth's dream come true.

Miraculously, the phone rang, and it was Thom. He had just gotten word that Celine had viewed the film and would allow us to capture their meeting. Could Basem and I get to the airport in forty-five minutes?

Getting through security at the airport is one thing; getting through security at Caesar's Palace is no small feat. There are signs posted everywhere: NO CAMERAS ALLOWED. Basem and I took a deep breath as we passed through the many levels of security with our video camera and boom microphone in tow. Meeting up with the Rormans in Celine Dion's hospitality suite was thrilling; the family sat huddled together on a massive white leather sofa as Celine, looking larger-than-life, entered the room.

Whether or not you are a fan of her music, Celine's talent is undeniable, and her song performance of "Beauty and the Beast" is iconic. However, what I was not prepared for is her extraordinary humanity. I sat in awe, holding the boom mic overhead and watching as Celine, who could easily have chosen to sit comfortably in the big white leather chair across from Beth and her family, instead chose to kneel on the floor next to Beth as she reached out to hold her hand. Celine spoke lovingly with Beth and shared her own insights while acknowledging Beth's admirable strength and courage.

The show started twenty minutes late that night, as Celine did not want to rush the visit in any way. The show was incredible, but the greatest moment occurred when Celine announced to the sold-out audience that she was dedicating the performance to her new friend, Beth.

"Wow, that's our mom," I heard one of Beth's boys say as they both beamed with pride. All I could think of was, "God bless Celine Dion," and thank you, Beth, for giving me my most profound brush with greatness.

Beth passed away on July 29, 2003. She will continue to live on in the hearts of those who loved her.

Basem Wasef, Beth Rorman, and me

Chapter 13

Of Mice and Men

During my tenure at The Walt Disney Company, I recognized that for the most part I was often the only woman in the room. By this, I mean to say there was a corporate culture that was mostly male dominated. In general, very few women were employed in creative capacities, and certainly none in the area of music production in animation. Yet I discovered that even the coarse threads of experience could create the appearance of something magical.

My experience working with Michael Eisner, chairman and CEO of The Walt Disney Company, reminds me of the children's story "The Emperor's New Clothes." For some reason, Michael seemed to surround himself with people who would tell him what he wanted to hear. Some were better at it and less obvious than others. Everyone responded in exactly the same way to the man who the media reported was micromanaging Disney to the extreme.

Many silently questioned Michael Eisner's motives for hiring his friend Michael Ovitz to run the Disney studio. Michael Ovitz, founder of the top talent agency Creative Artists Agency (CAA), represented himself as a true Hollywood insider. I could not help but be impressed by Mr. Ovitz's ability to do six things at the same time. I jumped at any opportunity to observe him firsthand and would do my best to find a seat next to him at our meetings. Just to witness him working his BlackBerry into a frenzy while participating in the meeting was a sight to see. Within a few months of Michael Ovitz's arrival at Disney, I received a congratulatory note from him on my recent promotion. The announcement appeared in the *Hollywood Reporter*. The note meant a lot to me, and I certainly never received anything like that from Michael Eisner in the years I worked for him.

Participating in meetings with senior executives like the two Michaels was a privilege, but not for the faint of heart. There is nothing more sobering than sitting across the table from someone like Michael Eisner and never receiving a formal or informal introduction. No one spoke unless spoken to, and you were never to engage in conversation if you happened to share the same elevator.

However, one of my favorite moments occurred during a discussion regarding a proposed *Jungle Book* sequel. The two Michaels were there, and the discussion centered on voice casting and the availability of the voice talent from the original film. Michael Eisner asked if we had approached Phil Harris to reprise his role as the beloved character Baloo the bear. There was absolute silence in the room. No one wanted to respond for fear of making Michael look "uninformed." However, Mr. Harris had died some time ago. After a long pause, someone finally spoke up and said, "Mr. Harris is dead." Without missing a beat, Michael Ovitz banged the table with his fist and said, "That's okay, I can get him." Again, there was absolute silence in the room.

My *observational* brush with these two Disney corporate titans provided me with a unique educational perspective. At times, it challenged me to find and maintain my creative voice no matter how unwelcoming the environment may have been or whether or not I was the only woman in the room. That was certainly the case, especially when I had put my job on the line and stood up for my creative instincts while working on *Beauty and the Beast: The Enchanted Christmas*. Nonetheless, I appreciated the positive acknowledgment from senior management, especially during reviews for yearly bonuses.

Chapter 14

A Goofy Movie

Here is a trivia question you don't hear too often: "What do the legendary musical genius known as Prince and Disney's Goofy have in common?" The answer centers on the most rewarding and challenging film I have ever worked on as a music supervisor. *A Goofy Movie* was my first feature film, and there was a lot riding on its success. I wanted it to be great!

I met Jeffrey Katzenberg for the first time at a creative meeting for *A Goofy Movie*. Jeffrey had a reputation for being a "take no prisoners" executive. When he entered the screening room in a white T-shirt and jeans, he immediately commanded your attention, and though his appearance was casual, his demeanor was not.

There was a brief discussion before the screening. Director Kevin Lima explained we were about to view a leica reel sequence from the film that included a song demo. A leica reel is a type of storyboarding device and the most preliminary way of viewing artwork with recorded sound. Jeffrey Katzenberg's input was clear, concise, and direct, and I never forgot it. He said, "The key to the success of great storytelling is making sure that the characters express real emotions and are believable. . . . Humor is important, but you can always punch up the laughs later. The real challenge is to make sure your story has heart."

When the lights came up, there was no further discussion. Jeffrey merely uttered the word "wipeout," and in a flash, he was gone.

Jeffrey's reaction made it clear we had work to do. It was definitely time to regroup from our *executive* BWG.

The sequence we had shown to Jeffrey involved Goofy's nemesis, Pete. Director Kevin Lima decided he wanted a darker, slightly more menacing tone for Pete. He said he felt that the original Pete was too much of a cartoonish oaf, and suggested that we could make the transition for Pete's character through song. As an example, Kevin referenced the song the black crows sang in *Dumbo* called "When I See an Elephant Fly." He also suggested that we approach Tony Award winner Bill Finn, the Broadway composer of *March of the Falsettos*, to see if he would be interested in writing it. Kevin had eclectic taste in music, and I loved that he was willing to take risks, but even Bill Finn's agent seemed surprised by the casting interest.

The next thing I knew, I was on a flight to New York to meet with Mr. Finn. He lived in a high-rise apartment on the Upper West Side. The apartment was small and compact. As I entered, I was trying not to draw attention to the fact that I noticed Mr. Finn's Tony Award for *March of the Falsettos* was lying on its side in the middle of his coffee table, surrounded by a growing collection of empty Chinese food boxes, chopsticks, and dirty dishes. I stopped myself from fixing his Tony Award.

My plan was to listen to the song Mr. Finn was working on and leave with a song demo. Unfortunately, this was a decidedly very low-tech situation as I entered what I thought was a recording studio. It was, in fact, a bedroom. In the corner next to the window was a beat-up upright piano, the kind with cigarette burns on top of the keys. I looked around for a place to sit while making room on the corner of the unmade bed. Bill sang with reckless abandonment. I found myself captivated by this bear of a man and his peculiar-sounding singing voice. Bill Finn's bizarre brilliance was evident from the first note he played.

Unfortunately, his gospel-like song "Born to Be Bad," with its strange syncopated beat, never made it into the movie. Disney executives, including Jeffrey, did not think the song was melodic enough, which may have been true; but in my opinion, it was nonetheless inspired.

Evidently Mr. Finn, considered an autobiographical text writer, had suffered a near-death episode and required brain surgery. After surviving the experience, he decided to write a Broadway musical and called it *A New Brain*. Mr. Finn's eccentricity provided not only one of my most *eclectic* BWGs but also one of my strangest and mostly deeply personal musical theatre experiences as well.

There was a growing trend at Disney of putting pairs or teams together in the hopes of creating musical magic as Howard Ashman and Alan Menken had done. Walt Disney Television Animation attempted to do that by hiring Grammy Award–winning songwriter Tom Snow and pairing him with Broadway lyricist Jack Feldman. To describe them as the odd couple would be an understatement.

Tom Snow is somewhat of an enigma, a complex man with strong opinions and an uncanny ability to come up with hooky, iconic pop melodies. Jack Feldman, known in New York theatre circles, had achieved success as the lyricist who cowrote Barry Manilow's "Copacabana." Both men had previously worked on other Disney projects, although not together. Tom had contributed songs to the animated film *Oliver and Company*, and Jack had written lyrics to the songs in the live-action musical *Newsies*.

The pairing of Snow and Feldman produced the majority of the character-driven songs in *A Goofy Movie*, including the show-stopping opening number "After Today" and the heartfelt father-son song "Nobody Else but You." Bill Farmer as Goofy and Aaron Lohr, cast as the singing voice of Goofy's son Max, performed these songs. Aaron was a sweet kid who had a small singing part in *Newsies* and had just landed a starring role in the *The Mighty Ducks* movie.

David Z and Paul Peterson goofing around

We faced a number of challenges on *A Goofy Movie*, including changing score composers midstream. Joel McNeely left the project, Carter Burwell came on board but suddenly got very busy, and Don Davis helped fill out the score.

One of the biggest challenges I had was figuring out who could write the songs for Powerline, a central character in the film. His songs had to be believably cool and contemporary sounding in a timeless way. I reached out to songwriter Pat DeRemer. Pat and I worked together on many Disney projects. Pat wrote several songs for the *Totally Minnie* album as well as the theme to the Disney Sing-Along Songs home video series. I knew that Pat had a wonderful gift for pop hooks in his musical arsenal. He and songwriter Roy Freeland literally hit it out of the park, penning the two classics "I2I" and "Standout." For starters, Tevin Campbell, who was Prince's protégé and a Quincy Jones discovery, had agreed to sing the Powerline songs in the film. Next, finding the right music producer was critical, and that is what Prince and Goofy have in common. Getting Tevin's approval, I approached David "Z" Rivkin, the producer of

Studio interior of Prince's Paisley Park   Studio exterior of Prince's Paisley Park

the Fine Young Cannibals' hit "She Drives Me Crazy," "Purple Rain," and Prince's "Kiss," to see if he was interested in producing. I was thrilled when he said yes and suggested that we record the tracks at Paisley Park, Prince's studio in Minneapolis.

The drive to the studio seemed to take us through the middle of nowhere; then, suddenly, a white, modern-looking industrial complex appeared. We drove to the back of the building and up to a giant metal garage door. The experience was straight out of a Bond film as layers of doors opened. There I was, inside the inner music sanctum of the great Purple One's studio.

David Z, himself the epitome of cool, created an amazing track backed by the brilliant bass playing of Paul Peterson. Paul, a star in his own right, sang lead on the Prince-penned song "Nothing Compares to You" as the youngest member of The Family, a band formed by Prince.

Playbill featuring *Falsettos*, signed by Bill Finn   *Playbill* featuring *A New Brain*

Cool was evident everywhere you looked at Paisley Park. One of the studios had vivid graffiti art covering the walls. I had heard that the building had many secret exits and entrances, and I was especially interested in seeing Prince's legendary hidden boudoir. After a couple of days of recording, I got up the nerve to ask if I could get a tour of the complex, and I was not disappointed. Prince's hidden room was the highlight. It had a circular bed with the requisite number of mirrors on the walls and ceiling. It looked frilly with lots of satin material, but the thing that struck me was the number of framed pictures all over the room. I noticed that every picture was a picture of Prince, and he was the only one in the picture.

My trip to Paisley Park included a drive past Prince's house. Although the house itself was not visible from the street, I could see

A Goofy Movie, note by Bill Farmer (a.k.a. Goofy)

his windmill. Prince had built a windmill on his property that was fashioned to look like the one at the miniature golf and putt-putt across the street from Paisley Park. Remarkably, there it stood in all its glory. Apparently, after Prince had it built, he became unhappy with the view of it from his window. He had it turned to face a different direction and, in doing so, permanently rendered it non-functional—but it did look awesome.

As it turned out, *A Goofy Movie* had the right balance of heart and humor, along with terrific songs and score. Best of all, my brushes with greatness were not only colorfully animated but also bizarrely brilliant.

Chapter 15

Aladdin

Robin Williams returning as the Genie in the upcoming sequel to *Aladdin* was big news. But by the time the deal was sealed, the project *Aladdin and the King of Thieves* was well on its way to completion. The *Aladdin* television series had recast the Genie with Dan Castellaneta, a.k.a. the voice of Homer Simpson. Dan also voiced the Genie in the highly successful full-length direct-to-video *Return of Jafar*, and the script for another sequel was already under way. It was during that time I received a call from Disney executive Michael Lynton. In no uncertain terms, he made it clear that if Robin Williams was to come back as the Genie, I was to handle the situation with the greatest of professional diplomacy. Translation: "I am giving you notice: your job is on the line."

There were rumors abounding that Mr. Williams had been enticed back to Disney with the gift of a Picasso painting. True or not, Robin Williams's return was in fact a very big deal. Michael informed me that the best way we could maximize the Genie's role and Robin's return was to give him a couple of songs to sing. My job was to commission the songs, demo them, and arrange to have Mr. Williams ultimately record them.

At first I thought, what a tremendous opportunity for me to get to work with one of my all-time favorite actors. Then the other shoe dropped. I was told that the only time that Mr. Williams had to learn the songs was while he was on vacation with his family in Ireland. All I needed to do was find him an acceptable vocal coach, a rehearsal pianist, and piano at his hotel in Ireland.

So this is what *Mission: Impossible* is all about. I immediately wondered if it wasn't time for me to brush up my résumé. I knew that the key to this project was finding the right vocal coach. I started checking around and wondered who had worked with Jeremy Irons in *The Lion King*. The answer to my prayers came in the form of a lovely man named Ian Adams. I arranged to fly Mr. Adams and his young pianist protégé to Dublin from London. We met in the lobby of the hotel. I had confirmed that the piano in the penthouse where the Williams family would be staying had been properly tuned. We sat in the lobby bar, waiting for the Williams party to arrive. Mr. Adams was quite entertaining, sharing tales from his storied career. He felt confident that he and Mr. Williams would get on well, just as he had with Jeremy Irons. As we waited, I kept wondering if all this effort was going to be part of an ultimate boondoggle. Disney was sparing no expense in sending me to make the arrangements for Mr. Williams's convenience. I wondered if the effort mattered and if Mr. Williams would make the time we needed to teach him the two songs. After our brief introduction in the lobby, we arranged to meet the next day. For the entire week, Robin Williams devoted time each and every day to working on the songs. In fact, he seemed to really enjoy himself and made all of us feel appreciated.

However, the highlight of the trip happened by sheer coincidence. Several weeks before my trip to Ireland, in my capacity as a Disney music executive, I had a meet and greet with an Irish composer named Bill Whelan. I mentioned that I would be traveling to Dublin, and he kindly invited me to see a show he had written. I gladly said yes, provided there was time in my uncertain work schedule. I took down his information and decided to call him once I got to Ireland.

Unfortunately, Bill was in New York, but he offered to arrange a ticket to the show and said he would ask his wife to look out for me. As the taxi drove across town to a somewhat seedy looking area located near the fishing docks, I questioned the driver as he pulled up to what looked like a giant warehouse. "Are you sure this is the right address?" I asked. "Oh, yes," he said with certainty. "This show is very popular and completely sold out. If you don't mind me asking, how did you get a ticket to *Riverdance?*"

I had never seen anything like it, and I sat mesmerized the entire evening. I wished I had someone with me to share the experience. From the brilliant cast of dancers, who seemed to be flying through the air in a perfectly synchronized rhythm, to musician Eileen Ivers, whose fiddle bow appeared to catch fire with every note she played, *Riverdance* was spectacular. I went backstage to meet Bill's wife and gush my thanks for the extraordinary evening. Bill's music was nuanced and inspirational with an international flare. It was clear to me that *Riverdance* was a surefire hit, and I had another invisible thread weaving its way into my journey.

As I was preparing to leave the show that night, I saw Robin Williams. He was surrounded by the cast, posing for pictures and signing autographs. We waved at each other, and I boldly asked if I could bum a ride back to the hotel with him. He said sure. I was struck by how sweet and patient he was, literally taking time with each and every cast member. We had so much fun talking about the show on the ride back to the hotel. This was the first and only time I spent alone with him. I felt lucky to have had a bonding moment.

Weeks later, when we were in San Francisco recording the songs, we had a camera crew with us, filming the behind the scenes for the *Aladdin and the King of Thieves* electronic press kit. On our first night there, I suffered an injury when one of the directors accidentally closed the van door on my hand. I wound up spending the evening at the hospital having a partial cast made. The next day, unbeknownst to me, Robin filmed a get-well greeting for his friend "Bambi with the hurt paw." Needless to say, I was deeply touched.

Well, my BWGs on the *Aladdin* project were akin to the Genie granting me three fabulous wishes. How could I possibly top my experience of traveling to Dublin and working with Robin Williams?

The next stop on my *Aladdin* international tour was Melbourne, Australia, to record the main title. We hired Australian composer Bruce Rowland to arrange and conduct the theme song "Arabian Nights." The flight was eighteen-plus hours long. I tried to sleep on the plane, but it was really difficult. By the time we landed, the recording session had begun, so I went straight from the airport to Allen Eaton Studio. It was thrilling to walk in and hear members of the Melbourne Symphony Orchestra hard at work.

As a seasoned traveler, I knew that the best way to beat my jet lag was to try to trick my body into local time. This meant that I needed to stay awake at all costs, even though every bone in my body wanted to sleep.

I overheard one of the musicians talking about a concert they were going to that night, and I asked who was playing. They said Madonna. Well, I immediately knew that if Madonna's "The Girlie Show Down Under" couldn't keep me awake, then nothing could. The only problem was that the show was completely sold out. Remember Bill Meyers from my story about *Flashbeagle*? Well, it turns out that he was Madonna's music director at the time, and it's thanks to him I got to go to the concert and have an up close and personal experience. The venue was outdoors, and the stage was enormous. The coveted seats were folding chairs on the lawn in front of the stage. It was an absolutely dazzling show, and I had no trouble staying awake. I remember it was a misty evening, and as I sat looking up at the sky, I counted my lucky stars I was there.

Technically, however, seeing Madonna in concert would not be considered a BWG. My brush with Madonna happened in a soundstage at the Disney Studios several years before. I was producing a live-action / animated special for *The Wonderful World of Disney*, starring Donald Duck and John Candy. Our soundstage was next door to the one where Madonna was rehearsing. Use of the soundstage for her rehearsals was part of her compensation package for doing the movie *Dick Tracy*. The stage was a technological wonder of hydraulic lifts, and everything had to operate in perfect order. I used to sneak in to watch her rehearse. On this particular day, a group of us came out from the shadows and watched out in the open. All was going well until Madonna and her backup singers got their earpieces mixed up. Apparently, using the wrong earpiece is extremely painful. Madonna shouted "Stop!" and everything ground to a halt. She dramatically took out her earpiece and threw it across the soundstage, where it crashed on the floor, shattering into a million pieces. Madonna then turned to the group of us and pointed and yelled "Get out now!" So technically this was an *actual* brush, because it's not every day that you get yelled at by the Material Girl herself.

The third and last stop on the *Aladdin* worldwide express was recording the score in London. With composer Mark Watters at the helm, we arranged to record at AIR Lyndhurst, a recording studio that happens to be owned by Sir George Martin, who as their producer is considered by many to be the fifth Beatle. The acoustics in AIR Lyndhurst are world-class by any standard, mostly because it exists within the walls of a converted church. The ceiling can be hydraulically raised or lowered, depending on the size of the orchestra and the sound desired. Our orchestra comprised the principal members of the London Symphony Orchestra. Oh, what an amazing sound they made. I still get chills thinking about it.

Of course, we wanted to hear stories about the Beatles and Sir George. We grilled everyone we met, asking, "What's he like?" "Does he ever stop by the studio?" and "Is he still in contact with the remaining Beatles?" According to our engineer, Sir George doesn't frequent the studio unless he's working on a project. So you can imagine our surprise when, on our third day of recording, we had a visitor join us in the booth: Sir George Martin came in to observe.

He seemed sincerely interested in what we were doing and mentioned how much he enjoyed animation. At first I thought he was just being polite—but then I remembered the brilliance of *Yellow*

CLIENT				ASSISTANT		
FREQUENCY RUN				LEVEL REF TO.		
TITLE			TAKE	TO		FRO

Love to Bambi for marti x. Geoff

George Martin autograph

Submarine. Apparently he was keen on speaking to me about my experience of working with Robin Williams. Although Sir George was vague on the details, he said he was working on a project and wanted to approach Robin about singing a song. I later found out that he was working on *In My Life*, a CD of cover versions of Beatles songs.

After having kissed the Blarney Stone while in Ireland, I would like to think that my glowing endorsement of Robin Williams's work ethic helped to seal the deal for him and allay any of George Martin's concerns. Robin wound up recording the Beatles classic "Come Together" in a duet with Bobby McFerrin.

Me, our engineer, Sir George Martin, and Mark Watters

Chapter 16

The Other *Lion King*

Meeting Matthew Broderick for the first time at a New York recording studio was nothing short of unsettling. Of course, I was a fan of his and loved him in the 1983 film *WarGames*. I may secretly even have had a crush on him, so when he was cast as Simba in *The Lion King* and we were working on the sequel *The Lion King II: Simba's Pride*, I thought it was our destiny to meet. After we exchanged initial pleasantries, Matthew Broderick looked at me and said, "You're going to fire me."

I had gone to see him the night before in his Tony Award–winning Broadway show *How to Succeed in Business without Really Trying*, and I distinctly remember breaking out in a cold sweat the moment Matthew opened his mouth to sing. OMG! Why didn't I know he is a tenor?! In an instant, my heart fell into my stomach. I thought, how on earth would I be able to elicit a vocal performance from a tenor who needed to sound like the offspring of a baritone. Not just any baritone, but the son of Mufasa, voiced by James Earl Jones, the former voice of CNN, not to mention DARTH VADER.

How could I possibly fire Simba? And yet despite all my denials, it was as if Matthew was able to read my mind and sense my concern. The session was anything but fun or easy. Matthew was preoccupied with a personal issue involving his mother's health, and things just seemed to go from bad to worse.

Out of the blue, my newfound friend Gilbert Gottfried decided to stop by and surprise me at the studio. Gilbert and I had a lot of fun recording the songs that his character Iago sang in the *Aladdin* TV series and sequels. We often got together whenever I was in town. He brought along his friend Penn Jillette. I tried to explain that the session was not going well and I had to cut our visit short. All of a sudden and completely unprovoked, Penn Jillette started making fun of Matthew Broderick. Maybe he thought that Matthew was being difficult, and this was his way of showing support; regardless, I was mortified and feared that Matthew would overhear the tirade. After ushering them out the door, we finally finished the recording. Though the song was nearly cut out of the film, it ultimately remained, but not without a significant amount of music editing magic.

Relieved that the worst was behind me (or so I thought), I looked forward to the next day's vocal with Kathleen Turner, the star of several of my favorite films, like *Jewel of the Nile*, *Peggy Sue Got Married*, *The War of the Roses*, *Body Heat*, and the unforgettable Jessica Rabbit in *Who Framed Roger Rabbit*.

Ms. Turner had been cast as the evil lioness Zira, and she had a villainous song to sing. Arriving on time, she was an absolute delight. Though not a singer by training, Ms. Turner learned the song, and we got a couple of takes recorded before stopping for lunch.

Unlike the day before, everything seemed to be going well. However, after she returned from lunch nearly an hour and a half late, an uncomfortable exchange took place between Ms. Turner and our director Rob LaDuca. Ms. Turner went into the booth to sing, and something was clearly wrong. Suddenly she no longer sounded like she had before lunch; her intonation was completely off. No amount of music editing magic could save that performance.

The role of Zira was recast, and the song was eventually sung by *The Bob Newhart Show*'s beloved Suzanne Pleshette. Ms. Pleshette

Ernie Sabella (Pumba) and me

was by her own description "a bawdy broad who knows how to have a good time." I found her to be wildly warm and wonderful with a wicked sense of humor. She had a mouth that would make a sailor blush, and she said that "back in the day, I could drink any man under the table." Needless to say, the vocal session was colorful, and I would have to call this my *bluest* brush with greatness.

My *Lion King* brushes continued to be difficult. One of the lion cubs named Nuka was voiced by Andy Dick, and his character had a couple of lines in Zira's song. Rude and foulmouthed would be a fair description of Andy Dick's behavior that day in the studio, but what made him completely despicable was how he kept handling his crotch during the vocal session. He was so out of it that we had to take several breaks just to get the two-line performance recorded. Perhaps Andy Dick had fallen prey to Hollywood typecasting, because *Nuka* means smelly or stinky in Swahili. I'm sure there is a Dick joke in there somewhere. Thanks to Mr. Dick, I had experienced a new kind of brush: one I could have done without.

Top: director Rob LaDuca, Kathleen Turner, Tom Snow, and me; bottom: engineer James Twomey and Matthew Broderick

But all was not lost on *The Lion King II: Simba's Pride*. One of my brush highlights was working with the comic genius Nathan Lane. He came to the studio completely prepared and was remarkably serious about the work at hand. His self-deprecating asides had us all in stitches. When Ernie Sabella, who voiced Pumba, arrived, the two of them turned into the Odd Couple, trading barbs as they created their own form of Timon and Pumba pandemonium. I was grateful for our *hakuna matata* BWG.

Chapter 17

You're in the Music Business, Maybe You Know . . .

I am an admitted spa-aholic. It is a condition that developed many years ago after my first massage, and I have since traveled great distances for the best spa experiences. In fact, I was watching a television show called *Lifestyles of the Rich and Famous*, and it featured the top five spas in the world. I decided that on my next vacation, if ever I should take one, I would travel to Saturnia, Italy, the number two spa on the list. I thought that Bangkok, Thailand, the number one choice, was a little too exotic for a solo jaunt.

I chose Terme di Saturnia because I would be traveling alone, and I booked an all-inclusive week's stay. I flew into Rome, where an Italian driver, who spoke no English, met me at the airport. The car was prearranged, so I assumed he knew where to go. For nearly an hour and a half, he spoke to me in Italian. Strangely, I understood him, even though I do not speak Italian. I asked my mother about this, and she said that when I was a baby and we were living in New York, I was often in the care of my Italian family, who only spoke Italian.

We drove into the hills of Tuscany and arrived at what appeared to be a ranch compound. It was nighttime, and a foggy haze

115

surrounded the property. As I entered the main building, I remember the distinctive smell of sulfur. Within minutes of checking in, I discovered that I was the only American staying at the spa, and their only English-speaking employee would not be in until tomorrow. Through a series of hand gestures and words that sounded like "mangia," the waiter asked me if I was hungry. Despite the smell of rotten eggs, I nodded and said yes.

Entering the dining room, I spotted a table for one. This would be my table for the duration of my visit. A man seated at the head of the table next to me appeared to be blind. The woman with him had her hands full with a little boy who looked to be about five years old and a baby in a stroller. Their table was very active, and it seemed as if there was a constant flow of people stopping to say hello. I looked at the menu; it was in Italian. I could not understand it at all. I ordered by pointing to something on the menu I thought I recognized. The waiter smiled obligingly, but I am certain that my order must have been the entertainment for the evening. I inadvertently ordered seven courses. I did not want to appear impolite, so I kept eating and then finally begged them to stop bringing me food. Then, bless his heart, the chef prepared a special menu for me in English for the remainder of my stay.

The next day, I met the English-speaking concierge. We chuckled about my ordering disaster. She explained that Saturnia is a resort destination for Europeans, and I really was the only American there. She said she noticed that I was vice president of Music at the Walt Disney Studios and wondered if I knew one of the other guests also in the music business. She mentioned the name of a singer I didn't know, and told me he was very popular in Italy.

My room overlooked the healing waters of Saturnia. The lore surrounding the waters is that Saturn's bolt of lightning struck the ground and created the natural hot springs. According to legend, the appeal of the waters has to do with their medicinal properties, which I found hard to believe because of the ever-present film of gunk that floated on the surface. However, I will admit that I did feel oddly rejuvenated after spending time in the water. I am convinced that its power may have something to do with pigeon poop. I have never seen so many pigeons in my life, and they would spend hours on end flying back and forth from one side of the building to the other . . . making deposits in the healing waters.

On day two, I was in the hallway when I heard the most magnificent operatic voice. I assumed it was coming from the hotel's PA system. Then, suddenly, the voice stopped in midphrase, and I knew it was someone vocalizing. As it turns out, every day at around 4 p.m., I could hear this incredible voice coming from the room next door to mine. With book in hand, I sat quietly, listening to my own private concert.

My stay in Saturnia was indeed magical. The spa and treatments were the best I have ever had. The food at the restaurant was from a five-star menu. The people were warm and friendly. The town had a population of two hundred. I met all 199 residents, except for the one person who was away on holiday. The spa was located next to sunflower fields, and my daily walks were absolutely breathtaking. However, the thing that completely astounded me and offered a delightfully *unforeseen* encounter was that the blind man who worked in the music business happened to be the opera virtuoso Andrea Bocelli. At this point in his career, he had yet to become a global superstar, and he had yet to meet the extraordinarily talented Heather Headley. I would one day look back on this as another example of those invisible threads that link together the events in our lives.

Not all my *Lion King II: Simba's Pride* experiences were difficult. In fact, my work-related brush with Heather Headley led to a long and blessed friendship. Heather played the role of Nala, Simba's girlfriend, in the Broadway production of *The Lion King*. We actually met in Chicago during her rehearsals for Disney's *Aida*. Most Broadway-bound shows are workshopped outside New York. There are so many adjectives I could use to describe Heather's divinely guided talents, but her warmth and kindness of spirit are what made me know her as a friend.

When I first heard the demo recording of "Love Will Find a Way," I knew casting the duet would be easy as long as Heather sang the song. We paired her with the soulful recording artist Kenny Lattimore. "Love Will Find a Way" is the beautiful result of their duet, and it appears as the end title song on *The Lion King II: Simba's Pride* DVD.

I can't speak for Heather, but I can tell you the exact moment the bond of friendship took root. It was at 4 a.m. in a fountain in front of the Tree of Life at the Animal Kingdom in Florida. We were there shooting the music video for the song "Love Will Find a Way." As you can imagine, the shoot had a lot of moving parts, and I had never been to a Disney park in the middle of the night when it was closed. We had a limited time to get our shots before the sun came up and the park reopened. As tired, cold, and hungry as we all were, the director wanted one last shot by the fountain, which would surely get everyone wet. There was a moment of tension around this request, and then suddenly out of the silence came bursts of laughter as we collectively went for it. We huddled together afterward. I couldn't have been happier with the result and so grateful to my new friend.

Heather went on to win the Tony Award for her role in *Aida*, which was something Sidney Poitier and I had predicted standing together at JFK airport baggage claim. Heather's star was clearly on the rise when she was invited to perform as a special guest in concert with none other than Andrea Bocelli. I was thrilled when she asked me if I wanted to go to the concert.

As the lights went down, I made my way to my seat. I could not have sat any closer unless I had been a member of the orchestra. I was captivated by the sheer power and beauty of Mr. Bocelli's voice, and tears began to roll down my face. I thought I would burst open with pride when Heather joined him onstage and sang with her God-given gift of vocal grace and conviction. It was a truly transcendent experience.

Heather Headley and Kenny Lattimore   My Andrea Bocelli backstage pass

I don't know if she knew about my Andrea Bocelli brush at the spa in Saturnia when she arranged for me to meet her backstage. It somehow felt like more than a coincidence as I found myself, once again, in the presence of one of the world's best-known opera singers; only this time I knew who he was, and he was singing with my friend Heather.

Chapter 18

And the Award Goes to . . .

I had stopped watching television when *The Mary Tyler Moore Show* went off the air. I suppose it was a self-imposed protest, but I secretly related to Mary Richards, an independent, career-minded woman, and her lovable best friend, Rhoda, and I missed them. During the show's seven-year run, I watched every episode. This was way before binge watching; it was appointment television. I cheered when the show won its first Emmy Award in 1975, and cried when its last episode aired in 1977. For my generation, that series really made me aware of the power of television.

I love awards shows. I love watching the red carpet arrivals, seeing who is with whom and, of course, what they are wearing. It is one of my favorite guilty pleasures.

I will never forget the first time I went to the Emmys, in 1989. Excited by the opportunity to attend the forty-first annual Emmy Awards, I didn't care that I was a designated seat filler. Admittedly, there was nothing particularly glamorous about the experience. I was just thrilled and excited to be in the room. Being a seat filler is a nerve-racking job, because your sole purpose for being there is to ensure that there is a body in the assigned seat when the cameras are rolling. In between those long commercial breaks is a strangely choreographed ballet of bodies scurrying in and out of the auditorium. When you are not in a designated seat, you are waiting in a holding area, so the truth is that you never get to see the show.

The next time I went to the Emmys was a little different. I actually got to work on the show. The producer in charge of the "clip packages" hired me to research and log tapes for the segments that air with the announcement of each nominee. It was the fifty-third annual Emmy Awards in 2001, and Ellen DeGeneres was set to host. I thought maybe this time I would get lucky and actually get to sit in my own seat. Besides, I had remembered an earlier brush with Ellen DeGeneres that did not go well. It was 1998, and I had been sitting outside Dean Valentine's office (the former president of Walt Disney Television, ABC's parent company), waiting for a meeting that was clearly running late. I had one of those not-so great moments when a brush happens and you wish you were not there. This was one of them. I will never forget the look on Ellen's face as she left Dean's office and brushed by me. I found out later that she had just been told her sitcom *Ellen* was canceled.

With Ellen set as the Emmys host, I hoped for a "second chance" brush. The Emmys were scheduled to air in September 2001, but all that was to change when the horrific tragedy of the 9/11 terrorist attacks occurred. As our nation mourned, the idea of a Hollywood awards show became completely inappropriate. Of course, this meant that the Emmy Awards show to be hosted by Ellen was canceled.

Then, a couple of weeks later, without much fanfare, we got word that the show would go on. With Ellen still as host, the plan was to reconceive the show with an appropriately somber and respectful tone. Everyone worked night and day leading up to the date of the rescheduled show. No one was prepared for the news that came that morning: the United States had invaded Afghanistan, and our country was at war.

We all waited anxiously outside the Shrine Auditorium for news of what would happen next. Ellen was in the theatre rehearsing when word came down that the show was canceled for a second time. I happened to be outside the Shrine as Ellen exited the building, and once again, I saw a very unhappy look on her face. Again, not a great brush.

Then, on November 4, 2001, for security reasons the awards show moved from the Shrine Auditorium to a smaller venue in Century City. This made tickets hard to come by. On the day of the show, as luck would have it, I got an eleventh-hour call from my boss, letting me know that an extra ticket was available. Wow, I thought, I finally get my own seat . . . but it was not to be. Unfortunately, with the newly added levels of security, there was no way for me to get there in time to use the ticket.

Sitting in the comfort of my own home, I watched along with a global audience of 645 million people, in ninety-six countries outside the United States, as Ellen DeGeneres did a brilliant and wonderfully memorable job as host of the twice-canceled Emmy Awards show.

My work at Walt Disney Television Animation gave me the opportunity to become a voting member of the Television Academy. During the ten years I was head of music at WDTVA, we were nominated for or won Emmys for Outstanding Music Direction and Composition eight times. Attending the ceremony as a nominee is an entirely different kind of nerve-racking experience than the ones I had as a seat filler.

There were certainly invisible threads connected to my ultimate brush with Ellen DeGeneres. Even though I had two (less than pleasant) prior encounters with her, the third time really was the charm. My brush with Ellen DeGeneres finally happened at the 2004 Daytime Emmy Creative Arts Awards, six years after our first encounter. As an elected member of the Daytime Emmy Awards committee, I had a front-row seat next to multi-daytime-award nominee Ellen DeGeneres and her then girlfriend, Alexandra Hedison. Another Disney invisible thread: Alexandra is the daughter of David Hedison, who starred in the classic television series *Voyage*

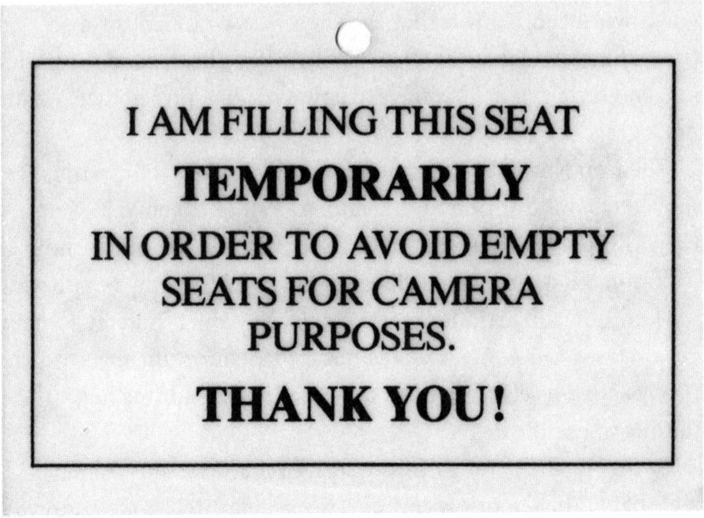

I AM FILLING THIS SEAT
TEMPORARILY
IN ORDER TO AVOID EMPTY
SEATS FOR CAMERA
PURPOSES.

THANK YOU!

I had to wear this badge at all times while I was in the auditorium.

to the Bottom of the Sea, and Ellen voiced the character of Dory in Disney's animated blockbuster film *Finding Nemo.*

Choosing this happy occasion, I approached Ellen and congratulated her on her nominations. The moment, captured in a sweet photo of the two of us, made for a happy ending after all.

For a music person like me, the Grammys represent the ultimate music business BWG experience. Attending the show provides a guaranteed firsthand sighting of the music industry elite. I could name names, but a sighting is not a real brush. I didn't have my first Grammy brush until 1990, when I was offered a chance to work on the show. I had to work at night so as not to interfere with my Disney day job.

I was hired to help research the images used as part of the opening film clips that ran behind Billy Joel as he sang "We Didn't Start the Fire." The song lyrics were all visual references to a catalog of headline news events that occurred during Joel's lifetime from March 1949 to 1989.

As a thank-you for a job well done, producer Phil Savenick offered me a pass to attend the show as a seat filler. The thought

Ellen DeGeneres and me

did cross my mind that I was now becoming a professional "SF." However, I also knew that I would have the ultimate experience of sitting among music's greatest talent, not to mention the best view of the stage.

The evening was a complete blur, and I was too overwhelmed to retain much of any memory except one. My seat assignment was in the center section of the orchestra at the Shrine Auditorium in the second or third row from the stage. I watched as Melissa Etheridge took the seat in front of me, and then k.d. lang appeared and crouched down to speak with her. As I was leaning over in an attempt to eavesdrop on their conversation, the lights suddenly started to go down, and everyone was scrambling to get to their seat. Out of nowhere, the person whose seat I was filling showed up, and I was stuck. I had no time to get up, so I had to crouch down on the floor in my gown. Just when I thought I could escape my awkward predicament, I managed to step on Gloria Estefan's foot, and she let out a holler. Thank goodness we were on a commercial break, because everyone looked around to see who had caused the

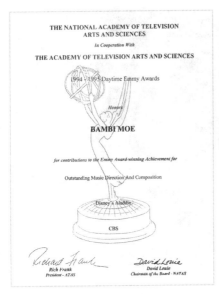

Emmy Award certificate for *Aladdin*

Cover of "The Last Show" script from *The Mary Tyler Moore Show*, signed by the cast

commotion. Completely embarrassed, I muttered my apologies to her, having what I would later recall as my least auspicious Grammy BWG.

In 1991, I ran for and won a seat on the board of the Los Angeles Chapter of the Recording Academy. By this time, I had become an active member in the music industry and was invited to participate on the NARAS television committee. A seat on that committee is highly prestigious and sought after for the backstage access alone, not to mention authorized entrance to closed-door rehearsals.

One of my most unexpected and intimate encounters occurred backstage at the Grammy Awards. I think of it as "intimate" because it happened in an elevator at Madison Square Garden and because so few words were exchanged. I was in a small group that included Bruce Springsteen.

I had read somewhere that "the Boss" does not like to sign autographs, but I figured I was not likely to be this close to him again,

Bruce Springsteen autograph in my Grammy   Sandy Melvoin and Luciano Pavarotti
Awards program

and I wanted to find some way to document the moment, so I asked for an autograph as I handed him my Grammy program. A feeling of panic ran through my body when I realized I didn't have a pen. The air in the elevator grew heavy, and my chest was pounding. With some brushes, all you have is a moment. The doors to the elevator were about to open, and I knew my chance of securing an autograph was about to exit. The Boss, seeing the look of sheer panic on my face, said, "Hey, anybody got a pen?" and all of a sudden five pens appeared out of nowhere. My program was signed, and the Boss was gone in a flash . . . and he didn't seem to mind being asked.

Most of all, I loved watching the dress rehearsal / show run-through. Anything can happen during rehearsals. Sometimes there is a palpable sense of magic in the air, and I vividly remember one of those times. I was sitting in the audience, in the dark, surrounded by larger-than-life-size posters used as seat markers with various celebrity names emblazoned on them. With only a few people in the

Photobombing Sting and writer Bruce Vilanch   Peter Max and me

theatre, Eric Clapton and Babyface walked onto the stage to rehearse and gave a heartrending performance of "Tears in Heaven." There wasn't a dry eye in the house; even the most hardened members of the tech crew shed a tear that day.

I witnessed one of Grammys' most infamous moments. It occurred thanks to Luciano Pavarotti. Billed as a rare appearance, the maestro was to perform on the show. Unbeknownst to all but a few, the reclusive Pavarotti did show up for his rehearsal. I have rare proof of his presence in the theatre that day: a picture I took of him sitting with my friend Sandy Melvoin. The press reported that Mr. Pavarotti fell ill early in the day and would not be appearing on the show. The press also reported that he missed rehearsal, which was not true either. Mr. Pavarotti's decision to pull out of the performance occurred no more than twenty minutes before the live broadcast was to begin. The show producers, in a last-minute effort to save the segment, approached Aretha Franklin, who graciously stepped in and sang

"Nessun Dorma." Without benefit of a rehearsal, Ms. Franklin literally blew the roof off the building with her larger-than-life rendition.

With a production credential in hand, I freely snapped candid photos of some of music's giants and may have photobombed a few as well, but the one photo and brush with greatness that meant a lot to me was with a nonmusical artistic genius.

I have a large poster collection that started back when I was a preteen living on Long Island in New York. It began with my collecting monthly calendars featured in *Newsday*, the local newspaper. I loved them because they were whimsical in design and reminiscent of the animation style used in the Beatles' *Yellow Submarine*. The pop artist who created them is Peter Max. I have many Grammy posters, but the ones I covet most are the two that Peter Max designed. Meeting Mr. Max backstage at the Grammys was a thrill!

Years later, thanks to a hard-earned bonus I received from my job working at The Walt Disney Company, I was able to purchase my first work of art, *Flower Blossom Lady*, by Peter Max.

Chapter 19

When Stepping in Pooh Can Be a Good Thing

When I was in a position to hire the songwriters for a new Winnie the Pooh animated feature, *The Tigger Movie*, there was only one team I had in mind: the Sherman Brothers. Without a doubt, Richard M. and Robert B. Sherman are the closest thing to what could be described as Disney royalty. It's hard to imagine the depths of musical talent that these two giants possessed. The word *genius* comes to mind. From "It's a Small World" to the Oscar-winning songs in *Mary Poppins* to "The Wonderful Thing about Tiggers" and the "Winnie the Pooh" theme, and countless others, the Sherman Brothers' songs are known to many generations of children around the world. What a privilege it was to hear the brothers' stories about working with Walt Disney; my immense gratitude extends far beyond my brush with their legendary greatness.

Though the Sherman Brothers didn't write the song "House at Pooh Corner," it seemed to me that a symbiotic connection existed between them and singer-songwriter Kenny Loggins, who did write it. I had an idea that their collaboration would produce something magical. Though I will never know with certainty, I suspect that up

Richard Sherman, Kenny Loggins, me, and Robert Sherman

to that point in time, neither Kenny nor the Sherman Brothers were aware of each other's collective careers. I respectfully approached all parties about the idea of writing an end credits song for *The Tigger Movie*. To this day, I get chills when I think about the song "Your Heart Will Lead You Home."

First of all, I have never been so much a part of the birth of a song. And I am honored that Kenny Loggins included me in the dedication in his CD booklet. Kenny, with guitar in hand, began a process I could only describe as divine inspiration. Over and over, he played the melody until it sounded just right. There I was, sitting knee to knee with Kenny as he set music to the lyric that he and the Sherman Brothers had sketched out earlier in the day. Not knowing how long the process would take, and not wanting to disturb the flow, I patiently sat there thinking, how can I tell Kenny Loggins that I have two tickets to the Greek Theatre to see Alanis Morissette that night? Never mind, I thought; this was an *extraordinary* brush with greatness, and I wouldn't miss it for the world.

Richard M. and Robert B. Sherman note and photo

I experienced so many genuinely magical moments during the years I worked at Disney. It would be almost impossible to pick one as the greatest. However, my heart will always remain somewhere in the Hundred Acre Wood. I have to put the endearing and lovable characters from the land of Pooh at the top of my list. Maybe it has something to do with Winnie the Pooh, Tigger, Eeyore, Piglet, Kanga, and Roo possessing equal amounts of childlike wonderment along with relatable human frailties. Or maybe another way of saying it is that there's a little bit of Pooh in all of us.

Chapter 20

Name That Toon and Tell Me Where It Was Recorded

For many years, I managed to fly under the Disney corporate radar. I was never politically motivated in my job or sought to get ahead by stepping on other people's toes; my reward was the satisfaction of working with some of my personal music heroes.

My private mission was to reinvigorate the career of some of the music industry's greats who may have been considered by some (but not me) to be past the height of their popularity. So when it came to casting and recording the vocals for our TV series theme songs, who better to sing the *Jungle Cubs* theme than Lou Rawls? Or the *Quack Pack* theme by Eddie Money? Or Mickey Thomas of Jefferson Starship, who decidedly rocked *The Mighty Ducks* theme?

Throughout my career, I discovered that the name "Bambi at Disney" grew to mean something. "The Velvet Hammer" was a nickname given to me by my colleagues and peers. I approached my work in a straightforward manner, but I always tried my best to exercise diplomacy. I grew to trust my intuition and relied on it, especially when work challenges centered on the fact that I was in charge and also the only female voice in the room. In truth I took no offense at the nickname and appreciated the respect afforded me in my career.

At first, talent would take meetings with me out of sheer curiosity, not believing there was a woman named Bambi who worked at Disney, and later because of my reputation for the award-winning work I produced. I had meetings with Richie Sambora, Marty Stuart, Trace Adkins, Marshall Crenshaw, Chely Wright, Wendy and Lisa, Julia Fordham, Jill Sobule, Jonatha Brooke, and many, many others—all with the intention of finding a project to work on together. I can see now that an invisible thread connected these incredible artists to various projects. Marshall Crenshaw recorded songs for *101 Dalmatians*, Chely Wright sang a song on *The Little Mermaid*, and Jonatha Brooke wrote and recorded the extraordinarily beautiful and timely "I'll Try" from *Return to Neverland*. I even got to meet the late, great genius Jim Henson when he was shooting *The Muppets at Walt Disney World*. Talk about a brush with greatness, and as a result, I am among the few on the planet with a personally autographed 8 × 10 from Mr. Rainbow Connection himself, Kermit the Frog.

One of the coolest *unexpected* BWGs I had was with Pat Benatar. I set up a meeting to discuss a song that we wanted Pat to sing in *An Extremely Goofy Movie*. When my idol and her husband and guitarist Neil Giraldo arrived at my office, Pat noticed the poster from our series *Pepper Ann* hanging on the wall, and much to my amazement, she started singing the theme song. With some pride, I told her I had coproduced it, and actress-singer Kathleen Wilhoite had sang it. Pat told me that the show was a personal favorite at her house. How cool is that? I think I must have blushed ten shades of red.

It can be pretty intoxicating to have your dreams come true, and mine often did. Was magic at work when I commissioned a chart-topping number one hit single? The project was a direct-to-video called *Mickey's Once Upon a Christmas*, and we needed an end title song that we could use to help promote it. I found out that Lyric Street Records, the now defunct Nashville-based Disney-owned record label, was planning to release a Christmas CD by a girl group called SHeDAISY. So I arranged a screening for the Osborn sisters, a.k.a. SHeDAISY, and explained that we had a difficult deadline. I hoped they had a song for our end title use that was already recorded. They loved the movie so much they went to work immediately and delivered the most creative, artistic version of the Christmas classic "Deck the Halls" I had ever heard—in fact, upon release it catapulted to number one on the adult contemporary charts. Literally a dream come true, and how could I not remember the comment I made to Michael Jackson about the challenges of making pop-friendly hit records for kids?

Looking back, I can still remember the first time I walked into a recording studio and felt intimidated by all the equipment. I didn't even know how to turn it on, let alone how to operate it. The twenty-four- or forty-eight-track mixing board, reel-to-reel tape machines, and a plethora of buttons, knobs, and screens were overwhelming. I had no idea where to sit or what to look at. That was 1981.

In the twenty years that followed, my Disney work took me all over the globe, and I spent a lot of time in recording studios. I went to the talent, wherever they were. The hours were long and often included weekends. I learned that the recording process is just that: a process. It takes as much time as it takes to complete the work. So many different variables can slow things down, mostly related to technology, and the job requires a great deal of patience and concentration. It was both rewarding and exhausting. I loved working in the studio and contributing to the creative process. I had the privilege and good fortune to work in world-class recording studios. Each and every studio has a unique history and an endless list of renowned artists who have recorded there. Much of this information is readily available via Google.

Earlier I described in some detail what it was like working at AIR Studios in London on the *Aladdin* project. There is something so magical about recording in a converted church. The church-like acoustics at Angel Studios, where we recorded some of *Beauty and the Beast: The Enchanted Christmas*, were extraordinary. Notably,

Kermit the Frog

Pat Benatar and me

there is no shortage of amazing studios in London, and perhaps the most well-known is Abbey Road . . . of course, made famous by the Beatles, and, yes, I took pictures with composer Mark Watters and music editor Dominick Certo in the iconic crosswalk in front of the studio. In Australia, we worked with composer Bruce Rowland on the *Aladdin* main title at Allen Eaton Studios in Melbourne and scored the series music with Mark Watters at ABC Studio in Perth. Overseas recording was more budget friendly, and as a result, we were able to record with larger orchestras. In New York, we recorded many song vocals from *The Little Mermaid* series at the Audio Dept. with engineer James Twomey and some of *The Lion King II: Simba's Pride* vocals at the Electric Lady Studios. In an earlier chapter, I described recording tracks for *A Goofy Movie* at Prince's Paisley Park in Minneapolis. Then there was the time I worked at a studio in Washington, DC, but I have blocked out the name—probably because I had a near-death experience on the way there, riding in a van with Joseph Shabalala and the members of Ladysmith Black Mambazo. The legendary South African performers, popularized

Kenny Thompkins (director), Lou Rawls, and me

by their work with Paul Simon on his *Graceland* album, were in America for a performance at the Kennedy Center, and I needed to record their vocals on our *Lion King II* tracks. The studio driver transporting us accidently drove the wrong way on a one-way street. We narrowly avoided disaster and were all clearly shaken. The group safely stepped out of the van and broke out in song. It was a beautiful moment to be sure, and they affectionately started calling me Bambalay from that moment on.

We recorded *Pooh's Grand Adventure* at Skywalker Ranch in Marin County. This world-renowned, state-of-the-art recording facility was built by filmmaker George Lucas as the headquarters for Lucasfilm and is considered a world-class filmmaker's retreat. Here's

Mickey Thomas and me

why: location, location, location. Skywalker Ranch is nestled in the hills off of Lucas Valley Road and maintains a vineyard, a lake, a barn with animals, and a spectacular garden of fruits and vegetables with an on-site restaurant. The area is private and secluded, and to work there, most creatives are invited to stay on the property. Each bedroom at the ranch is themed and tastefully decorated. I stayed in the Akira Kurosawa room, which had spectacular views from the window. Awakened by the sound of a rooster crowing in the distance, I never knew what kind of animal might be grazing outside my window.

Our home base was Los Angeles, and many of the studios we recorded in are located on studio lots. At Fox it was the Newman Stage, Paramount Stage M, Todd-AO at CBS Radford, the Eastwood Scoring Stage at Warner Bros., and A&M, now known as Henson Studios. There are so many others, all equally incredible, like Sunset Sound, Capitol Records, Evergreen, Jennifudy, Oh Henry, the Record Plant, and the list goes on. Again, all worth Googling for their history.

These places are all unique and yet the same in terms of purpose. I grew to love and respect, and have tremendous admiration for, the engineers, mixers, music editors, and assistants with whom I worked.

SHeDAISY and me

I had come a long way from my days of producing and editing story records, using a reel-to-reel quarter-inch tape machine and cutting tape with a razor blade.

However, in all sincerity, the most magical place of all was the Walt Disney Studios Stage A. That's what it was called when I worked there. In 2018 this historical orchestral stage was rededicated and renamed in honor of the Sherman Brothers and their musical legacy. It is now known as the Sherman Brothers Stage. Rumor has it that somewhere, hidden within the walls, is an endless supply of pixie dust. Given my magical Disney brushes with greatness, I have to believe it's true. I can't help but wonder if I had been sprinkled with pixie dust a long time ago.

Epilogue

There is no greater agony than bearing an untold story inside you.

—MAYA ANGELOU

Throughout the process of writing these stories about my brushes with greatness, I began to uncover the invisible thread that runs through the fabric of my life. I had been part of the magic. I had been a cast member at The Walt Disney Company during the '80s and '90s. I had the privilege of contributing my talents to a legacy of music and song. I was also that kid who was teased and bullied for having a funny name that connected me to the Disney Studios. It somehow made sense to me that Michael Jackson would want to meet the real live Bambi at Disney; after all, we shared a love for and interest in all things Disney. Robin Williams prioritized his work for Disney while on vacation with his family and bonded with each of us. Kenny Loggins and the Sherman Brothers were destined to meet somewhere in the Hundred Acre Wood, and they took me on their adventure. How could I not be grateful for the discovery of my future friends and extended family: Heather Headley, Susan Egan, Mark Watters, David Z, Rachel Portman, Sir Don Black, Desirée Goyette, Adam Berry, the Jefferds family, and my beloved Mickey and Minnie, Wayne and Russi.

The global pandemic that began in 2020 has affected everyone on the planet. Through loss and recovery, I have discovered many silver linings in my life, and with them new BWGs.

While clearing out the contents of an old steamer trunk, I made an interesting discovery. Next to a tiny keepsake wrapped in cotton, its special meaning now long forgotten, was a stack of VHS tapes and DVDs. When I saw the titles, a flood of old memories came to me as I journeyed back, only to find the past I had left so far behind.

One of the most important aspects to creating the music for Disney projects involves casting. In the case of animation, this would normally mean casting the voice actors. However, equally important is the casting of the songwriters for each project. This is an area that became particularly challenging as the Disney direct-to-video business was expanding, and many of the sequel titles under consideration were based on classic Disney feature films.

Holding the DVD box for *Lady and the Tramp II: Scamp's Adventure* in my hand, I noticed the omission of the names of the songwriters and the songs from the packaging. I remembered how that had bothered me, because it seemed to reflect the perception of the general value of music by those in charge at the time. Historically speaking, I find this particularly frustrating, because we had the privilege of pairing Academy– and Grammy Award–winning songwriter Norman Gimbel and Grammy Award–winning singer-songwriter Melissa Manchester, together for the first time, for this project. Personally, I think that is worth remembering.

I instantly recalled another first as I scanned the box cover for *The Hunchback of Notre Dame II*. Jennifer Love Hewitt, cast as Quasimodo's love interest Madellaine, wanted to write and sing a song for the film, which was something she had never done before. Jennifer was thrilled when I managed to line up top record producer Rob Cavallo to record the song. Tucked in the box was a picture of the three of us in the studio.

I am fairly certain that William Shatner's recorded performance of the end title song "To Infinity and Beyond" from the *Buzz Lightyear of Star Command* DVD was a first—and perhaps a last.

Me, Rob Cavallo, and Jennifer Love Hewitt

Finally, I would be remiss if I didn't mention recording Robert Goulet at a studio in Las Vegas singing "Green Tambourine" for the music video on *Recess: School's Out*. That experience was a first for all of us on many levels.

As we prepared this book for publication, I regularly called my editor Lisa McMurtray. Sharing the experience of my latest brush remembrances with her created unique bonding moments. I realized that the real joy of a BWG is sharing it with someone else.

I hope that by my sharing my stories, you will be inspired to share your own and discover life's joyful threads.

About the Author

Photo courtesy of the author

Bambi Moé is a highly accomplished creative executive with extensive experience in children's and family programming. As the former Vice President of Music for Walt Disney Television Animation, she spearheaded the music for well-known animated films and television series such as *A Goofy Movie, Beauty and the Beast: The Enchanted Christmas, Aladdin: Return of Jafar, Hercules,* and *The Little Mermaid* TV series, to name a few.

Before her twenty-year career at Disney, she was the Director of Development and Production for Rhino Records Video. She later founded and co-owned Courgette Records, a multi-Grammy-nominated independent record label. Moé created and hosted PBS-TV's *Composers on Composing* for Los Angeles' public broadcasting station, KLCS-TV, in addition to contributing to their music-centric programming.

Moé is currently a strategic adviser for the children's edutainment initiative MC and Friends. She continues to provide her creative expertise to a legacy project celebrating the life of Philo Taylor Farnsworth, the inventor of broadcast television.

Moé developed and taught a course curriculum for the music business studies program at California Polytechnic University, Pomona, and holds a teaching certificate from the Los Angeles Unified School District.